T0268407

Hidden
MALTA

VINCENT ZAMMIT

INTRODUCTION

Merħba (Welcome) to Malta!

Hidden Malta gives visitors an opportunity to explore the hidden gems of the Maltese archipelago. Beyond the thriving main streets that attract the tourist crowds, there are so many other places waiting to be discovered, including churches, small museums, and places to eat, where you can meet and connect with locals.

Although small in size, Malta has a wide range of cultural, architectural and historical treasures due to its strategic location in the middle of the Mediterranean. The many naval powers that occupied Malta left their mark on the archipelago's topography as well as on its population over the centuries, making it a fascinating melting pot of pagan, Christian and Islamic history, with its own unique identity.

During the rule of the Knights of St John, various artists and architects visited Malta. The most famous, of course, was Caravaggio and two of his canvases are still on display in Malta today. One of these is also the artist's largest and the only one he ever signed.

Hidden Malta also guides readers to Malta's many annual festivals and traditions, with historical re-enactments, wine, beer and music festivals, as well as food fairs held in various parts of the islands throughout the year.

Hidden Malta, your ticket to an unforgettable experience!

ABOUT THE AUTHOR

Born and raised in Valletta, Vincent Zammit joined the Museums Department in 1978 as a guide, participating in various archaeological excavations among others. In 1993, he became a lecturer at the Institute of Tourism Studies (Malta), which trains Malta's future tourist guides. A visiting lecturer at the University of Malta since 2008, Vincent now takes guests with special interests and small intimate groups on tours. Over the years, he has attended various international conferences where he has conducted workshops and delivered papers on guiding techniques, alternative tourism, cultural tourism, and Maltese history. Vincent is also a regular contributor to Maltese and international publications and has published various books on the history and culture of Malta in Maltese and English.

In this alternative guide to Malta, Vincent pays tribute to the islands that he knows intimately, choosing to highlight places that are not well-known or frequented by visitors to Malta, giving them the opportunity to discover these hidden gems and the Malta that he loves.

The author would like to thank all the people who played an instrumental role in the writing of this book, providing tips and suggestions as well as support, such as Joseph Mizzi, Dirk Timmerman, and the photographer Joseph Galea as well his wife Anna and his daughter Victoria-Melita.

HOW TO USE THIS BOOK

This guide lists over 360 places to visit and things to do in Malta or things to know about the island, that are presented in different categories.

We have included practical information such as the address, the phone number and the website if available. For the purpose of this guide Malta has been divided into six areas – five regions plus the capital city, Valletta – each with its own map that can be found at the beginning of the book. Each address is numbered from 1 to 369 and the area is provided in the description. When you're looking for a secret in Valletta, its number will help you to locate the address on the map. The other five maps have legends consisting of a list of the numbered secrets located in that region, to help you get oriented. More detailed maps can be obtained from the local tourist information centre or from most good hotels. Or you can use your smartphone to locate the addresses.

The author wishes to emphasise that cities and countries are always subject to change. Malta and Valletta are no different in this respect. A delicious meal at a restaurant may not taste quite as good on the day that you visit it or a small museum with irregular opening hours might be closed when you knock on the door. Some locations might be difficult to find and sometimes you may need to exercise some patience but ultimately you may come across something wonderful. This personal and subjective selection is based on the author's experience, at the time of compilation. If you want to add a comment, suggest a correction or recommend a place, please contact the editor at *info@lusterpublishing.com*, or get in touch on Instagram or Facebook: *@500hiddensecrets*.

DISCOVER MORE ONLINE

Hidden Malta is part of the internationally successful travel guide series called *The 500 Hidden Secrets*. The series covers over 40 destinations and includes city guides, regional guides and guides that focus on a specific theme.

Curious about the other destinations? Or looking for inspiration for your next city trip? Visit THE500HIDDENSECRETS.COM. Here you can order every guide from our online shop and find tons of interesting travel content.

Also, don't forget to follow us on Instagram or Facebook for dreamy travel photos and ideas, as well as up-to-date information. Our socials are the easiest way to get in touch with us: we love hearing from you and appreciate all feedback.

the500hiddensecrets

@500hiddensecrets   #500hiddensecrets

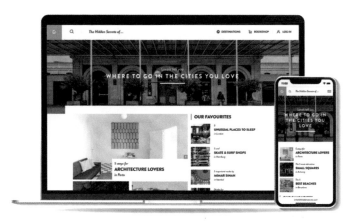

MALTA

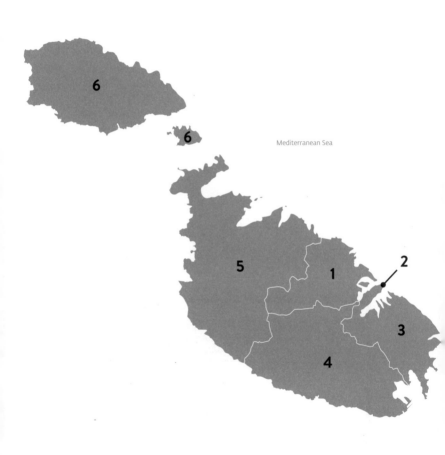

Mediterranean Sea

1 CENTRAL MALTA

2 VALLETTA

Fort Tigné

St Elmo Bay

St Elmo Heritage Building

Marsamxett Harbour

Fort Manoel

212

49 175 92

368

Marsamxett St

Republic St

Merchants St

121 173
176 355
357 346 243 51 332 143 181 53
91 72 14 4 287
302 77 68 80 356 56 264
348 70 120 81 329 297 359
114 353 1 279 350 154 282 358 355
241 9 94 7 58 St Ursula St 364
107 330 13 161 63 Lower Barrakka Gardens
351 292 256
153 116 142 12
138 286 Quarry Wharf
10 86
25 105 347 184
132
11 Upper Barrakka Gardens

St Lucea St

South St

Melita St

Hastings Garden

St Paul St

122

Lower Barrakka Gardens

Grand Harbour

The Mall

Herbert Ganado Gardens

Xatt Pinto

St Anne St

King George V Recreational Grounds

Fort St Angelo

Gardjola Gardens

5 NORTHWEST MALTA

Ċirkewwa

Mellieħa

Qawra

St Paul's Bay

Burmarrad

Naxxar

Manikata

Mġarr

Mosta

Mtarfa

Rabat

Mdina

Dingli

6 GOZO & COMINO

Żebbuġ

Għarb
Għasri

Marsalforn

GOZO

Xagħra

San Lawrenz

Kerċem
Victoria

Nadur

Qala

Xlendi
Munxar

Xewkija

Għajnsielem

Sannat

Mġarr

COMINO

OUR LADY OF MELLIEHA ICON

ART *and* CULTURE Ⓐ

Art in
UNEXPECTED PLACES

1 **BRONZE AGE DAGGER**
NATIONAL MUSEUM OF ARCHAEOLOGY
Republic St
Valletta
+356 2558 4712
heritagemalta.com

Among the amazing collection of items on display at the National Museum of Archaeology is a Bronze Age dagger, created 3500 years ago. The bronze and bone dagger, which was found in a cave, is one the most impressive finds from this period. In addition to the bronze blade, the dagger has an elaborately decorated bone handle. Other items were found nearby, implying metalworking in the area.

2 **OUR LADY OF MELLIEHA ICON**
MELLIEHA SANCTUARY
Pope's Visit Square
Mellieħa
Northwest Malta
+356 2152 3449
geo.io/en/Sanctuary_of_Our_Lady_of_Mellieħa

At the Mellieħa Sanctuary a painting on the rock represents the Virgin with the Christ Child on her lap. One of the oldest traditions is that Saint Paul's companion, the Evangelist Luke, painted this when they were shipwrecked in Malta in 60 AD. However, it has since been assessed by art historians that the icon dates from the 13th century. The composition is typical of Byzantine Marian icons during the late 13th and early 14th centuries. There is another Madonna, in Mdina's Cathedral of Saint Paul, which is said to have been painted by Saint Luke. This probably dates from the Middle Ages, however.

3 ALBRECHT DÜRER COLLECTION

MDINA CATHEDRAL
MUSEUM
St Paul's Square
Mdina
Northwest Malta
+356 2145 4697
metropolitan
chapter.com

The Mdina Cathedral hosts a rich collection of historical artifacts. Your ticket to the cathedral can also be used to visit the museum on the other side of the square. Interestingly enough, the museum houses an impressive collection of woodcut and copperplate prints as well as lithographs by the German Renaissance artist Albrecht Dürer. Of note are a series of images relating to *The Life of the Virgin* and *The Small Passion*, a sequence of images on the Passion and Death of the Lord.

4 OUR LADY OF DAMASCUS ICON

GREEK CATHOLIC
CHURCH
132A Archbishop St
Valletta
+356 2123 7872
greekcatholic
malta.com

Behind the President's Palace stands a small church dedicated to Our Lady of Damascus. This is the church of the Greek Catholic community, which arrived in Malta in 1530, bringing their prized possession, the icon of Our Lady of Damascus, with them. The panel painting, which probably dates from the 12th century, represents the Virgin Mary embracing the Child Jesus, an image of love and piety. This is considered the oldest painting in existence in Malta.

5 MATTIA PRETI'S LARGEST PAINTING

ST LAWRENCE
PARISH CHURCH
91 Saint Lawrence St
Vittoriosa
Southeast Malta
+356 2182 7057

During the 38 years that he lived and worked in Malta, the Italian artist Mattia Preti received several commissions for paintings for various baroque churches on the islands. The largest canvas that he ever executed can be found in the Collegiate Church of Saint Lawrence in Vittoriosa. *The Martyrdom of St Lawrence* measures four metres by six metres. Preti painted this *chiaroscuro* work when he was 75 years old.

6 MATTIA PRETI PAINTINGS

ST CATHERINE
PARISH CHURCH
Republic Square
Żurrieq
South Malta
+356 2164 2010

The parish church of Żurrieq houses six canvases by the renowned 17th-century Italian painter, Mattia Preti. *Il Calabrese*, as he was also known, spent a number of years in this village where he owned a summer residence. The collection includes the magnificent titular altarpiece, *The Martyrdom of St Catherine*, as well as another imposing canvas representing Saint Andrew, the patron of fishermen.

7 POLIDORO DA CARAVAGGIO

ST JOHN'S
CO-CATHEDRAL
St John's St
Valletta
+356 2122 0536
stjohns
cocathedral.com

The Knights of Malta, or the Order of Saint John built Valletta in the 16th century, envisioning it as a cultural centre in Europe. St John's Co-Cathedral was built as an emblem of their faith and is one of the top churches to see on the Maltese islands, with an amazing art collection and interior. In addition to ceiling paintings by Mattia Preti, the Co-Cathedral is also home to a painted crucifix by the 16th-century Mannerist artist Polidoro da Caravaggio (not to be confused with Michelangelo Merisi da Caravaggio, on which more later). Originally this work of art was located in Vittoriosa (Birgu), the Knights' first settlement. The highlight of the collection is painting of the *The Beheading of St John the Baptist*, in the Oratory, the largest work by Caravaggio and the only one to bear his signature.

A

8 SILVER ALTAR STATUES

MDINA CATHEDRAL
St Paul's Square
Mdina
Northwest Malta
+356 2145 4697
metropolitan
chapter.com

Amongst the amazing treasures in the Cathedral Museum, there is also a set of 15 silver statues which originally embellished the main altar of St John's Co-Cathedral, Valletta. The work of the Roman silversmith Antonio Arrighi, they originally stood in St John's conventual church but were donated to the Co-Cathedral in the 18th century. When Napoleon's troops arrived in 1798, they looted the churches, searching for silver to mint coins to pay the soldiers. In an attempt to prevent the loss of these statues, the church paid a ransom on two occasions, saving one of the greatest silver treasures of the 18th century in the process.

9 SLEEPING LADY

NATIONAL MUSEUM
OF ARCHAEOLOGY
Republic St
Valletta
+356 2558 4712
heritagemalta.org

Head to the National Museum of Archaeology to see one of the most prized possessions from prehistoric Malta in a little dark room. *The Sleeping Lady* is an exquisite clay figurine from the Neolithic period, representing a woman sleeping on a couch, with a distinct hairstyle and skirt. This was unearthed in the underground complex of the Hal Saflieni Hypogeum.

Places for
CONTEMPORARY *art*

10 SPAZJU KREATTIV

ST JAMES CAVALIER
**Pjazza Kastilja /
Pope Pius V St
Valletta
+356 2122 3200**
kreattivita.org

Set within a 16th-century fortification, Malta's national centre for creativity hosts several art exhibitions and performances throughout the year. There are various spaces for exhibitions, cultural events, as well as a small theatre, ideal for small audiences. The massive interior blends well with the modern installations.

11 VICTOR PASMORE GALLERY

ST JAMES
COUNTERGUARD
**Vjal Nelson
Valletta
+356 2550 3360**
*patrimonju.org/
fpm-blog-victor-
pasmore-gallery*

The Central Bank of Malta possesses a number of original works by the British abstract artist Victor Pasmore. The bank joined forces with the Victor Pasmore Foundation to set up a permanent exhibition, highlighting the paintings and constructions that he created during his stay in Malta. A few earlier works have been added, to provide more of an insight into Pasmore's artistic practice.

12 VALLETTA CONTEMPORARY

**15–17 East St
Valletta
+356 2124 1667**
*valletta
contemporary.com*

Valletta Contemporary, the brainchild of local artist Norbert Attard, strives to bring internationally acclaimed exhibitions to Malta in addition to being an project for the Maltese contemporary art scene. The art gallery and exhibition space is located in Valletta's lower east end in a 17th-century warehouse.

Singular **S C U L P T U R E S**

---

13 CHRISTMAS CRIB
ST FRANCIS OF
ASSISI CHURCH
Republic St
Valletta
+356 2123 4019
sanfrangisk.com

In St Francis of Assisi Church a small crib is set up, with a detail that is not usually seen in other cribs. To the side of the traditional Nativity scene, there is a small grotto representing the cave in which St Francis originally recreated the birth of Jesus and the first creche near Rieti in Italy. The small figurines are dressed differently than the other ones in the larger Nativity scene. You can find it in the corridor leading to the church's convent, which is also worth visiting.

The Nativity is a common tradition in Malta, with people setting up Christmas cribs in their home and even in public places during the Christmas period. While pasturi figures are sometimes bought ready-made, others prefer to buy original pieces from local artisans.

14 MIRACULOUS CRUCIFIX
ST MARY OF
JESUS CHURCH
St John's St
Valletta
+356 2122 7570

The St Mary of Jesus Church in Valletta houses a devotional life-size crucifix, a 17th-century work of art by the Sicilian sculptor Fra Innocenzo da Petralia. Legend has it that the artist woke up one morning to find that the detailed head of the Christ was complete. This crucifix very rarely leaves the church but is on display throughout the year in its dedicated chapel. There are other similar crucifixes in churches around Malta.

15 COLONNA MEDITERRANEA
Roundabout at
Carmel St and
Triq San Tumas
Luqa
South Malta

The multi-coloured ceramic column, known as the *Colonna Mediterranea*, is located on a roundabout close to the airport. The abstract landmark created quite a controversy over its phallic appearance. However, the local artist who created it, Paul Vella Critien, maintains that it was inspired by ancient art.

16 THREE CROSSES
Off Triq Ħaż Żabbar
Triq il-Bidni
Marsaskala
Southeast Malta

A very singular and unique street religious sculpture can be found in the countryside, close to a small church, in the hamlet of Bidni. The memorial consists of three crosses, in relief, that have been affixed to a stone wall. Around the three crosses there are various symbols associated with the Passion of Christ. Various legends abound about why these crosses were set up here. In all probability, they were erected for public devotion.

A

17 TWIN FIGURES

ĠGANTIJA
PREHISTORIC TEMPLES
Triq Otto Bayer
Xagħra
Gozo
+356 2155 3194
heritagemalta.org

This statue, which was unearthed at the Xagħra Stone Circle, is the only prehistoric statue of its kind in Malta to feature two seated figures. There is debate about whether they are male or female, but they are similar to other Neolithic figures found in Malta. Both the figures wear a pleated skirt, while one of the heads is unfortunately missing. One is holding a smaller version of the figures, perhaps a doll, while the other clasps a bowl. Their hair is long. The couch on which they are seated is elaborated and decorated with spiral designs and dashes of red ochre.

18 WHITE SHADOWS MONUMENT

Tower Road
Sliema

Strolling along the Sliema waterfront, you will run into many families on their morning or evening stroll, enjoying the scenery and the sea breeze. This contemporary monument on the promenade evokes these families and other passers-by. Conceived by Richard England, this marble monument is a sculpture of cut-outs of human figures, with light falling through the figures. The shadows change according to the season and the time of the day.

19 LOVE MONUMENT

St George's Road
St Julian's

What is Love? According to Richard England, love is a reflection, and it cannot be seen and/or felt all the time. This is the meaning behind a contemporary monument that overlooks the water at Spinola Bay. The large marble monument features a cut-out of the word 'love' but the letters have been inverted. In order to read the word, you have to look at the reflection on the sea but you can only read it when the water is calm, implying that love is not always present.

STREET ART

20 CHARACTERS
Corner of
Hompesch Road
and Vjal Kottoner
Fgura
Southeast Malta

At one of the main intersections of this town, two large empty walls have been painted over. One of these is behind a busy bus stop, and the artist decided to paint a number of people waiting for the bus, including the young people, old age pensioners, workers, and so on that you would expect to find at this bus stop. The other wall, across the street, features various portraits of people.

21 **ENVIRONMENT**
Triq Bellavista
San Ġwann
Central Malta

The collaboration of a collective of street artists (SeaPuppy, Emoon, Twitch, IELLA and LANGER) has added colour to a white wall along a busy thoroughfare. The idea behind the decoration of this wall was the environment. It features landscapes, a running horse, and a woman blowing dandelions, among others.

22 **SKATE PARK**
M A Vassalli Road
Msida
Central Malta

A roundabout in the middle of one of the busiest intersections, close to the University of Malta, has been turned into a skate park, and artists have covered the walls with colourful street art scenes featuring figures and popular characters from their own cultural background. There is no real connection between the artworks, but they do highlight the diversity of the artists.

23 MARITIME GRAFFITI

CATHEDRAL OF
THE ASSUMPTION
**Cathedral Square /
The Citadel
Victoria
Gozo
+356 2155 4101**
*gozodiocese.org/
churches/parishes/
katidral*

Many of the churches in Malta have ship graffiti on their outer walls. These graffiti might refer to a vow made by a sailor, or even the crew of a galley, swept up in a storm, or attacked by pirates. The art implies that they survived their ordeal and is a mark of their gratitude. Look closely at the outer walls, and you will notice different types of vessels. Gozo Cathedral has several of these incised graffiti.

24 WHITE ROCKS

**Baħar iċ-Ċagħaq
Pembroke
Central Malta**

An abandoned holiday complex has become a legal graffiti wall where artists can flex their skills. The walls overlooking the main road and the interior of the buildings are full of very diverse artworks. Some of these murals cover the entire walls of the block of apartments, while others were created inside the buildings.

S M A L L *and* U N U S U A L *museums*

25 **NUMISMATIC COLLECTION**
CENTRAL BANK
OF MALTA
Castille Place
Valletta
+356 2550 0000
centralbank
malta.org

In the lobby of the Central Bank of Malta, you can see an interesting collection of coins and paper money. Coins were introduced in Malta during the Carthaginian period, towards the end of the 5th century BC. The earliest piece on display dates from around 400 BC and features Tanit, a Carthaginian goddess. The following period is well represented with Roman coins, with a more elaborate finish. The collection displays coins from all the different periods of Malta's millennial history, some of which attest to the artists' exquisite workmanship.

26 **CLASSIC CARS**
MALTA CLASSIC
CAR COLLECTION
Tourist St
Qawra
Northwest Malta
+356 2157 8885
classiccarsmalta.com

Walking through a museum collection of classic cars, many people are often surprised to see such a wide variety of well-kept and beautifully restored cars, such as a 1955 Jaguar, Fiats, Fords and several other classics. The well-designed display provides visitors with an interesting experience. To make your journey back in time even more captivating, the museum has added a collection of antiques and memorabilia from the forties, fifties and sixties, to put the collection into context.

27 QUARRY

LIMESTONE HERITAGE
Triq Mons.
M Azzopardi
Siġġiewi
South Malta
+356 2146 4931
limestone
heritage.com

The only natural resource that is in abundant supply in Malta is limestone, the stone that is used extensively by the construction industry. Stone is quarried, and this place provides a unique insight into what a quarry looks like from within, and how stone was excavated and transported during the previous centuries. There are various tools on display, in addition to explanations and films about this centuries-old craft. A good place to visit and relax.

28 POSTAL HISTORY

MALTA POSTAL MUSEUM
135 Archbishop St
Valletta
+356 2596 1750
maltapostal
museum.com

This newly opened museum provides an insight into Malta's rich postal history. The display includes a fully functional post office, with the old furniture included. The timeline of historic milestones starts in the 16th century, with the Order of St John in Malta, and the museum traces postal development throughout the following centuries, with stamps, drawings and other interesting items associated with local postal history.

29 MARITIME MUSEUM KELINU GRIMA

16 Parish St
Nadur
Gozo
+356 2156 5226

A small museum which was only opened in 1999, after a man named Kelinu Grima donated his extraordinary collection of maritime memorabilia to the parish of his village. The museum boasts photos and many other items that were donated by some of the officers and British admirals stationed in Malta at the time. Also on display are several letters associated with the island's maritime history, besides other items that Grima collected from ships stationed in Malta.

30 AVIATION MUSEUM

Ta' Qali
Attard
Central Malta
+356 2141 6095
maltaaviation
museum.com

The first airfield was built in Malta at the start of the 20th century and was used by both the British Royal Air Force and Fleet Air Arm. Since then, several airfields have been built in Malta, including this civil airfield at Ta' Qali. This is also where the Aviation Museum is located, close to the former airfield, using several of the airfield's hangars. There are several airplanes, and parts of aircraft on display, a remarkable collection for aviation enthusiasts. This is one of those specialist museums that is always a pleasure to visit. Highly recommended.

31 MUSEUM OF TOYS
POMSKIZILLIOUS
TOY MUSEUM
10 Triq Ġnien Xibla
Xagħra
Gozo
+356 2156 2489
gozotoymuseum.com

This small privately owned museum in an old building at Xagħra is home to the collection of Susan and Edwin Love, a British couple from Devon. It started with one doll but now includes a variety of toys, some of which are quite old. Among the most interesting items are a number of large doll houses, with the various rooms and furniture included, a popular toy with well-to-do families during the 19th century. You can also see a number of figurines, that are traditionally used in Maltese Christmas cribs, some of which are the work of an early 20th-century Neapolitan artist.

30 AVIATION MUSEUM

32 OLD PRISON

Cathedral Square /
The Citadel
Victoria
Gozo
+356 2156 5988
heritagemalta.org

Gozo's oldest surviving prison is open to the public, offering visitors an opportunity to walk through the narrow passages and see the cells. The place is well-kept, and it also provides an insight into prison life, with a number of informative panels explaining the different sections of the prison. Illustrious inmates include a French knight, called Fra Jean de Valette, a future Grand Master and the hero of the Great Siege of 1565. The Order of St John used this prison for rowdy and disruptive members of their order. It also has an interesting collection of wall graffiti, the work of the inmates. The prison was still in use till the second half of the 20th century.

33 POLICE MUSEUM

St Calcedonio St
Floriana
Southeast Malta
+356 2122 4001
police.gov.mt

This museum is located at the Police Headquarters and relates the history of Malta's Police Force, as well as displaying several interesting items used by the police throughout the years. The displays include guns, uniforms and other paraphernalia associated with the Police Force. An interesting section depicts some of the most notorious local homicides, with original weapons and photos from the crime scene. Not for the squeamish.

Art to feel **CLOSE TO GOD**

---

34 **GHARB PARISH MUSEUM**
Church St
Għarb
Gozo
+356 2155 6129
gharbparish@
onvol.net

This recently opened museum is located in Għarb Parish Church. The display includes items created by the island's early Punic, Arabic and Jewish inhabitants, while the main exhibits are of a more religious nature. Also on view is an extensive display of church silver, which is mainly used for the main religious feasts, as well as vestments and other documents pertaining to the history of the parish. The museum also has a small collection of works by local and foreign painters. A small but interesting museum.

35 **HEART OF GOZO – IL-ĦAĠAR**
St George's Square
Charity St
Victoria
Gozo
+356 2155 7504
heartofgozo.org.mt

This museum about the history of the Church and its surroundings was established close to the Basilica of St George, Victoria. The permanent collection includes several excellent pieces, such as religious vestments, paintings and church silver, which is usually used to decorate the basilica on feast days. The works on display span a number of centuries and artistic styles. Some were produced by foreign craftsmen, while others are by local artists. A small and interesting intimate museum. Occasionally they also host contemporary exhibitions.

Il-KARRU TAL-MEJTIN TAL-PESTA (1813)
Maħdum minn Gioacchino Xerri
(Matul din il-pesta mietu 4500 persuna,
52 minnhom minn Ħaż-Żabbar)

PLAGUE HEARSE (1813)
Made by Gioacchino Xerri
(During the plague 4500 people died, 52 of
them from Ħaż-Żabbar)

36 ST JOSEPH ORATORY

Triq Nestu Laiviera
Vittoriosa
Southeast Malta
+356 2182 7057

An interesting museum located within an 18th-century Oratory, with different historical and cultural artefacts associated with the Vittoriosa parish and city. Keep an eye out for the smaller items in the display cases, such as the tongs that were used by priests during plague epidemics to avoid touching plague victims while administering Communion. Don't forget to check out some of the books on display. Besides being old and interesting, they also belonged to local historical personalities. There is a small chapel next to the Oratory, where you can see the hat and sword used by the hero of the Great Siege of 1565, Grand Master Jean de Valette. Definitely worth the detour.

37 ŻABBAR SANCTUARY MUSEUM

Triq is-Santwarju
Żabbar
Southeast Malta
+356 2182 4383

Malta's first church museum, dating from the 1950s, is still open to the public and was even recently refurbished. The museum has a nice collection memorabilia from nearby Żabbar Parish Church, dedicated to Our Lady of Graces. Besides the various religious items on display you can also see some votive paintings here, dating from the early 17th century onwards. Part of the local maritime heritage, they reference the many mishaps, events and storms that sailors used to experience. Another interesting item on display is a wooden cart or plague hearse.

AIR FORCE MONUMENT

HISTORY ⬭

C E M E T E R I E S *worth a visit*

38 **ST LAWRENCE CEMETERY**

St Edward St
Vittoriosa
Southeast Malta
+356 2182 7057

Lying amongst the massive 17th-century fortifications surrounding the Three Cities, this cemetery was established at the beginning of the 19th century, after an explosion killing more than 200 people, led to lack of space within the church's crypt. Besides the locals, this is also the last resting place of Thomas McSweeney, an Irish seaman with the British Navy, who was executed in 1837, after being court-martialled. His tomb is visited by those who believe that he was wrongly executed and who believe that they have received graces through his intercession.

39 **CAPUCHIN FRIARS CRYPT**

F. S. Fenech St
Floriana
Southeast Malta
+356 2122 5525

Beneath the first Capuchin Church and Friary established in Malta in 1588, there lies an interesting crypt. For burials, the Capuchin Friars used to mummify the corpses of the departed, and bury them standing up in alcoves, cut into the rock. A wooden plank would be installed before the necks of the corpses, in order to keep them standing. The friars were buried in their religious habit. Today a modern fibreglass figure is used to show how the friars were originally buried. A number of multi-coloured marble tombstones, commemorating some of the lay persons who are buried here, are exhibited.

40 CAPUCCINI'S NAVAL CEMETERY

Triq San Leonardu
Kalkara
Southeast Malta
+356 9989 1837
cwgc.org

Kalkara Military Cemetery, as it's officially called, is managed by the Commonwealth War Graves Commission, and it is the final resting place for more than 1000 casualties from the two World Wars. There are also civilian burials, and a Japanese Naval Memorial. This memorial commemorates naval personnel who died in Malta during the First World War, as Japan had allied itself with Britain. This is one of the places that are visited by Japanese tourists while in Malta.

41 IMTARFA MILITARY CEMETERY

Triq Buqana
Attard
Central Malta
+356 9989 1837
cwgc.org

Another cemetery managed by the Commonwealth War Graves Commission. This has more than 1400 civilian and military burials, dating from the First and Second World Wars, amongst others. Some of the graves still feature bomb damage, as the cemetery lies close to one of the airfields that were used during World War II. Six members of Prime Minister Sir Winston Churchill's team who lost their lives in a plane crash, while on their way to the Yalta Conference in 1945, are also buried here.

42 MSIDA BASTION CEMETERY

Vincenzo
Dimech St
Floriana
Southeast Malta
+356 2122 5952
dinlarthelwa.org

This served as a Protestant burial ground between 1806 and 1856. The principal burials were of British personnel stationed in Malta, both civilians and servicemen. There are also some Maltese buried here, including the author Mikiel Anton Vassalli, the father of the Maltese Language. Some of the neo-classical monuments are impressive. The various symbols used on the tomb decorations are noteworthy. The cemetery has been beautifully restored and turned into a peaceful garden.

43 TA' BRAXIA CEMETERY

Independence St
Hamrun
South Malta
+356 2122 5952
dinlarthelwa.org

This is a burial ground for civilians, which was taken into use around 1850. It also has a small Jewish section. Originally it was intended to be a multi-faith burial site, but the local Roman Catholic authorities opposed this idea. Designed by the local architect Galizia, the cemetery continues to be used until this day. There are a number of interesting funerary monuments. A memorial chapel dedicated to Lady Rachel Emily Hamilton-Gordon, built in a neo-Gothic and neo-Romanesque style, dominates the cemetery. Some of the tombstones also feature Masonic symbols.

44 OTTOMAN MILITARY CEMETERY

Triq il-Marsa
Marsa
Southeast Malta

Commissioned by the Ottoman Empire in the second half of the 19th century, this cemetery was designed by Galizia, a Maltese architect. The architect built it in an Orientalist and Romantic style, the preferred architectural style of the time. Galizia was honoured by the Ottoman authorities for the design of the cemetery. The small mosque within the cemetery was used for Friday prayers, before a proper mosque was built in Malta. Turkish prisoners of war from World War I are buried here, as well as Muslim servicemen members of Commonwealth countries. Today, this cemetery falls under the responsibility of the Turkish Government.

45 WIED GHAMMIEQ CEMETERY

Triq Santu Rokku
Kalkara
Southeast Malta

This somewhat forgotten cemetery was used during the cholera epidemic of 1837, which ravaged the island. The victims buried here were the hospitalised elderly who were transferred to nearby Fort Ricasoli, with the intention of benefitting from the sea breeze. Unfortunately, more than 850 people died, and they were hurriedly buried in an adjoining field. Their remains were later exhumed and reburied in a more orderly way. Eventually a small chapel was erected in the 1920s. Due to the belief that some of the inmates were buried alive, locals started to regularly visit this cemetery to pray for their repose. Religious services are still held here on Sundays and public holidays.

44 OTTOMAN MILITARY CEMETERY

45 WIED GHAMMIEQ CEMETERY

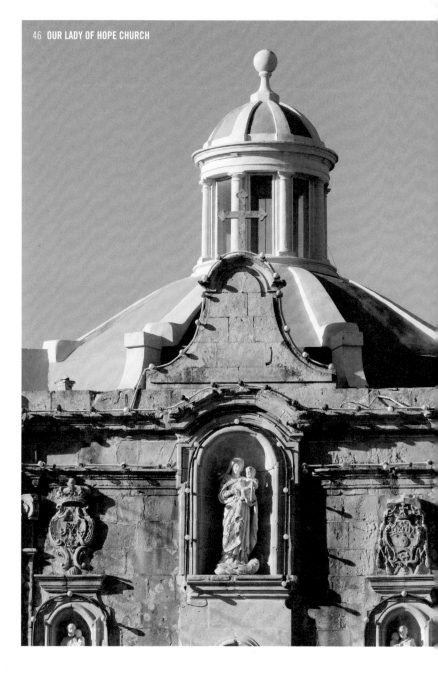

Intriguing **CHURCHES**

46 **OUR LADY
OF HOPE CHURCH**

Triq l-Isperanza
Mosta
Northwest Malta

A small, well-proportioned baroque church lies on the edge of a valley, which is associated with a story of a young country girl, who while trying to escape from marauding pirates, entered a small cave while praying to Our Lady for deliverance. Although the pirates managed to reach the entrance of the cave, they did not bother to enter as a large web sealed off the entrance. This led them to believe that the girl could not have entered the cave, as the web would have been broken. The girl later started to raise money in order to build a church in lieu of thanks. Beneath the present church, there is still a small cave, which supposedly is the same cave where the girl took refuge from the pirates.

47 OLD PARISH CHURCH OF ST CATHERINE OF ALEXANDRIA

Triq San Girgor
Żejtun
Southeast Malta
+356 2169 4563

Located on the outskirts of the town, this medieval church was used as a lookout for the surrounding coasts. In 1614, it was attacked and severely damaged, and this was one of the reasons why it was abandoned, and a new larger church was built closer to the village centre. About 50 years ago, during maintenance, a sealed passage was discovered within the thick walls. At the end of the passage, the workers discovered a heap of human bones. The church is also interesting for its architecture, and for having one of the earliest domes in Malta.

48 SANCTUARY OF THE IMMACULATE CONCEPTION

Triq il-Kunċizzjoni
Qala
Gozo
+356 2155 6684

Towards the end of the small village of Qala, you will find the cemetery, next to a church. The story goes that a hermit named Karrew was forced to escape from Malta, because the locals were fed up of hearing him admonish them for their sins. To escape he placed his cloak on the sea, and climbed on it, thus demonstrating that he was a saintly man. But the locals were not interested. After spending some time on Comino, he is said to have settled here, where he eventually died. After entering this well-decorated church, you will see steps to your left, leading into a small rock-cut chamber, where the remains of this saintly hermit are kept. The church still attracts a lot of devotees.

FOLLIES *and* FANCIES

49 **HOUSE NAMES**
Republic St
Valletta

When walking along the streets of Maltese towns, you will notice that many houses have a name next to their doorways. While most of the houses have official house numbers, others still go by their name. These names are either personal, with the owners using a combination of their names, or else the home would be placed under divine protection, with the name of a saint or even an image. Other names were simply chosen according to the owners' taste.

50 **LA RUOTA**
NATIONAL ARCHIVES
OF MALTA
Triq L-Isptar
Rabat
Northwest Malta
+356 2145 9863
*national
archives.gov.mt*

The previous medieval hospital, Santo Spirito Hospital, still has a window, with a revolving platform, where unwanted babies could be abandoned, to be taken into care by the hospital authorities. This window is known as *La Ruota*, the wheel, as it allows the mother to place her unwanted child in the window, then rotate the wheel, upon which a bell would ring inside the hospital. A screen prevented the people inside the hospital from seeing who abandoned the baby. The child would then be taken in and raised by the authorities. Abandoned boys would be trained in a trade, while girls were taught crafts associated with womanhood. Today the building is home to the National Archives.

51 **7TH OF JUNE MONUMENT / SETTE GIUGNO MONUMENT**

St George's Square
Valletta

A large bronze monument, commemorating the events of 7th of June 1919, dominates St George's Square. At the end of World War I, several workers found themselves unemployed, while food was still either scarce or too expensive. Street protests in Valletta, combined with requests for more political freedom, led to a number of clashes between the crowds and British soldiers, during which four men were unfortunately killed. Eventually a monument was installed in the main cemetery outside Valletta, and this public monument was erected in order to keep the memory of these people alive. The 7th of June is one of the national holidays of Malta.

52 GRAND MASTER VILHENA STATUE

**St Anne St
Floriana
Southeast Malta**

The public bronze monument to one of the 18th-century Grand Masters of the Order of St John, António Manoel de Vilhena, dominates a small square in Floriana. The statue was originally located in the parade ground of Fort Manoel, a fort built thanks to his generosity. The statue was a gift by a knight, who was taken to court by the widow of the sculptor, for payment owed. The statue was transferred to a square in Valletta in the 19th century, then moved to another location in Floriana, before finally ending up in the place where it stands today.

52 GRAND MASTER VILHENA STATUE

53 SHOE SCRAPER
OUR LADY OF
PORTO SALVO AND
ST DOMINIC CHURCH
Merchants St
Valletta

Various large buildings have two metal strips next to their doorways allowing guests to clean the mud off their before entering. You can see such shoe scrapers at the entrance to Our Lady of Porto Salvo and St Dominic Church in Valletta. In the old days, the streets were full of mud and dust and so it was imperative that you entered the church with clean shoes. You can find such shoe scrapers on many buildings.

54 SMALL WINDOW AND KNEELING STONE
CHURCH OF OUR LADY
OF THE ANNUNCIATION
Annunciation St
Rabat
Northwest Malta

When walking in the countryside, you will encounter several small churches, some looking as if they have been abandoned and forgotten. And yet certain religious feasts are still held in some of these churches. You may even come upon a church that is open and decorated for the feast day. When these churches are closed, there is still an opportunity to say a prayer in front of them. This church has two small windows, one on each side of the door, and a kneeling stone in front. This offers the possibility for a passer-by to stop, kneel, and say a prayer, while looking towards the main altar through the window.

55 EYES ON LUZZUS
Triq is-Sajjieda
Marsaxlokk
Southeast Malta

Take a close look at the bows of the colourful *luzzus* (fishing boats) in Marsaxlokk Bay, the largest fishing village in Malta, and you may see that they all feature an eye. These are believed to be a tradition from the Phoenician times, and they are referred to as the Eye of Osiris or Horus. They are meant to provide divine protection against any mishaps while out on the open seas.

56 SUNDIAL

St Paul's St
Valletta

There are many sundials all over Malta. Most of these sundials are on public buildings, others are on private dwellings. In Valletta, you can see a sundial, dating from 1695, on the old University building. The dial features hour lines from 5 am to 3 pm. This was one of the largest non-government buildings in Valletta, a Jesuit church and the forerunner of the present University of Malta.

57 VICTORIAN AGE POST BOX

Pjazza ta' l-Assunta
Żebbuġ
Gozo

Although Malta's postal history goes back to the 16th century, it was only during the 19th century that Malta was to have its first postal stamp. During the second half of the 19th century, the Malta Post was established, and it continued to increase its presence in various parts of the islands. The first letter boxes, with their distinctive red colour, were put up in various localities, mainly next to police stations. This letter box is still located near the village police station, dating from the Victorian era.

58 CHRISTMAS SHOP

JOSEPH CALLEJA
St Lucia St
Valletta
+356 2123 7018
jcalleja.com

Christmas is a time for festivities and for decorations – at home and in public space. But as this shop can attest, people do not just buy Christmas items in December. As is the case in so many other European cities, a Christmas shop provides enthusiasts with the option of buying decorations and other materials associated with the festive season, year-round. The Maltese tend to come here to shop for the figurines that are used to decorate Christmas cribs, representing the Nativity.

59 **ELEPHANT TUSKS**

GHAR DALAM CAVE
AND MUSEUM
Għar Dalam St
Birżebbuġa
South Malta
+356 2165 7419
heritagemalta.org

One of the most important cave discoveries is that of Għar Dalam, a cave near Marsaxlokk Bay. Upon excavating the cave floor, in the second half of the 19th century, the archaeologists discovered remains of a number of extinct animals, including elephants. These European species had moved south, escaping the cold, and finding themselves on islands, became smaller, thus evolving into dwarf species. Within the Għar Dalam Cave and Museum there are tusks of elephants of varying sides. Others remains that were found here include hippopotami, brown bears, wolves, and foxes.

60 **GALLEY ALTAR**

WIGNACOURT MUSEUM
2 College St
Rabat
Northwest Malta
+356 2749 4905
wignacourt
museum.com

One of the prized possessions of the Wignacourt Museums is the wooden portable altar used on galleys of the Knights of St John while at sea. These altars did not require a lot of decoration, as their main function was to provide a place where religious services could be performed. They were made to hold the chalice and other religious items in place, even during rough seas. This altar can actually be closed, looking very similar to a toolbox. Very few examples have survived the passage of time, even though there used to be one such altar on each of the galleys of the Christian fleets.

61 GRAFFITI

INQUISITOR'S PALACE
Main Gate St
Vittoriosa
Southeast Malta
+356 2182 7006
heritagemalta.org

Most people tend to be fascinated by the many prison cells at the Inquisitor's Palace. Equally noteworthy are the inscriptions that have been scratched into the walls of these cells by the prisoners that were held here. While some of these graffiti are limited to the name of the individual, others include numbers, a rose, a crucifix, and even Arabic script. There is also a small sundial, placed next to a window, to be used by the warden, while supervising the prisoners in the exercise yard below.

62 ROTUNDA CHURCH / MOSTA PARISH CHURCH

Triq il-Kbira
Mosta
Northwest Malta
+356 2741 8368
mostachurch.com

The massive dome that dominates the village and the whole surrounding area has an interesting history. Besides the story of the bomb that pierced the dome during World War II without exploding, there is also the interesting story of its design. The church design was not approved by the local Church authorities, as it was deemed not sufficiently Catholic. This also explains why the Bishop of Malta did not attend the stone-laying ceremony, thus publicly showing his disapproval. The church took more than 27 years to be completed, and it was built around the older 17th-century church, before the latter was demolished to make way for the newly completed massive Rotunda.

63 NELSON'S HOOK

**St John's St c/w
Merchants St
Valletta**

There is a metal hook, stuck into the wall of the old Castellania, the old Law Courts of the Knights of St John, at the corner of St John's Street with Merchants Street. The function of this hook is still a mystery. Some say that it was used to hoist one of the large bells of St John's Co-Cathedral. Others maintain that it was used to hoist prisoners on the corner pillory. Another option is that it was used to hoist prisoners while kept in a cage and left suspended in mid-air to the ridicule of the public. It later became part of the British naval myth, when Nelson managed to pass through the hook. Since that time, it has been known as Nelson's Hook, and whomever manages to pass through the hook will be guaranteed a successful naval career.

63 NELSON'S HOOK

64 SHORELINE BOLLARDS

Xatt il-Forn
Vittoriosa
Southeast Malta

When they arrived in Malta in the early 19th century, the British military authorities found many obsolete iron cannons. Instead of disposing of them, they installed them along the shores of the Grand Harbour and other harbours, to be used as bollards by the various vessels that plied the harbours of Malta. Although no longer in use, you can still find many of these bollards along the shores, some of which are still used by smaller crafts.

64 SHORELINE BOLLARDS

65 **OUBLIETTE**

FORT ST ANGELO
**The Great Siege
of 1565 St
Vittoriosa
Southeast Malta
+356 2540 1800**
heritagemalta.org

Under the Knights of St John, Fort St Angelo was also used as a prison. Some of the most notorious prisoners were also imprisoned in a disused well, known as the guva or *oubliette*. This cell could only be accessed through a trapdoor in its ceiling. One of the most famous prisoners to be confined here was the infamous artist Caravaggio before he eventually escaped. There are various inscriptions and names scratched into the walls of this grim prison, reflecting the desolation and despair that the prisoners must have felt.

66 **PLAGUE HEARSE**

ŻABBAR SANCTUARY
MUSEUM
**Triq is-Santwarju
Żabbar
Southeast Malta
+356 2182 4383**

Unfortunately, Malta suffered several outbreaks of plague over the centuries. Burial of the dead was always a problem, as nobody wanted to take the responsibility for transporting the corpses to their burial. At some point, prisoners were promised freedom if they helped to transfer the deceased to their last resting place. The bodies would be transported in a covered cart or hearse. You can still see such a hearse, the only one of its kind, at the Żabbar Sanctuary Museum, a church museum with several artistic treasures.

67 **PORTABLE ALTAR**

INQUISITOR'S PALACE
**Main Gate St
Vittoriosa
Southeast Malta
+356 2182 7006**
heritagemalta.org

A superb portable altar is on display at the Inquisitor's Palace. Noble families often owned such wooden altars. These pieces of furniture could be placed in a corner of a room. The cabinet would be opened in case of a religious service, transforming it into a proper altar with all the necessary items for the celebration of the service. This is one of the best kept portable altars that are to be found in Malta.

Curious **TALES**

68 **CLOCK TOWER**
GRAND MASTER'S
PALACE
**Republic St
Valletta**

In the small courtyard within the Grand Master's
Palace stands an 18th-century clock tower, which
was inaugurated in 1745. The clock is known as the
Moors Clock, due to the bronze figures of Moors
that flank the bell. In the 19th century, following
a complaint from a British Governor's wife, the
clock had to be modified so that it would stop
ringing during the late evening and the night.
The clock still dominates Prince Alfred's court.

69 **MALTESE CROSS**

The eight-pointed cross is generally referred to
as the Maltese Cross. In fact, its origin has nothing
to do with Malta. It was the symbol that the Order
of the Knights of St John used during their stay
in Malta between 1530 and 1798. Due to their
association with the islands, and the famous
victory during the Great Siege of 1565, the eight-
pointed cross became synonymous with Malta.
The eight-pointed cross is also the symbol of one
of the Italian principal Maritime cities, namely
Amalfi, and for that reason the same cross is also
found on the Italian Naval flag.

68 CLOCK TOWER

69 MALTESE CROSS

70 LORENZI HOUSE

Old Theatre St
Valletta

In June 1798, a large French armada, under the command of Napoleon Bonaparte, landed in Malta capturing the islands from the then defunct Order of the Knights of St John. Napoleon then continued his journey to Egypt. In the meantime, the French garrison sought to control the islands and impose their rule. A few weeks later, however, the Maltese revolted, and the French garrison ended up blockaded behind the fortifications of the Valletta harbours. Plans were immediately made to open the gates. One of the ringleaders was a retired Corsican seaman called Guglielmo Lorenzi, who lived in Valletta. Unfortunately, the plot was discovered and Lorenzi was one of several conspirators who were executed in front of the former Grand Master's Palace, in Valletta.

71 NEANDERTHAL TOOTH

GHAR DALAM CAVE
AND MUSEUM
Ghar Dalam St
Birżebbuġa
South Malta
+356 2165 7419
heritagemalta.org

During the excavations of Ghar Dalam, the cave where a large number of extinct animal remains were discovered, a tooth was discovered, prompting the archaeologists to state that it showed Neanderthal traits. This suggests that the earliest inhabitants of Malta lived here during the Palaeolithic period, and that they were of the Neanderthal species. In recent years this has been disputed. Discussions and academic studies are still both in favour and against this theory.

72 MALTESE FLAG

PRESIDENT'S PALACE
St George's Square
Valletta

Tradition has it that when the Norman Count Roger invaded Malta in 1091 and succeeded in defeating the Arab overlords, he gave the white and red colours of his family's coat-of-arms to the local people as a sign of affection. In fact, there is no documentary evidence to suggest this. However, during late medieval times, the white and red colours seem to have been adopted as the colours of the local governing body, known as 'universitas', which was located in Mdina and in the Cathedral of Malta. Today these are still the colours of the city of Mdina, whereas Malta has added the George Cross, an honour bestowed on the islands and its inhabitants by King George VI in 1942 for their bravery during the continuous attacks by the Axis alliance during World War II.

72 MALTESE FLAG

73 EXILES BEACH

Tower Road
Sliema
Central Malta

Why is this part of the rocky shoreline between Sliema and St Julian's known by this name? Soon after the Russian revolution, a number of Russian notables managed to escape and make their way to Malta. They settled in the immediate area, and during the summer months this is where they used to go and enjoy the summer breeze and swim. There used to be a few wooden changing huts as well. From this time onwards the area became known as the Exiles beach.

73 EXILES BEACH

Enigmatic **MONUMENTS**

74 **AIR FORCE MONUMENT**

King Edward VII
Avenue
Floriana
Southeast Malta

At the entrance of Valletta, there are a number of monuments. One of them commemorates the airmen who lost their lives during World War II while defending the islands. The base of the monument lists the names of the known airmen whose lives were lost. At the top of the column there is an eagle, with its wings pointing straight up, instead of being widespread, indicating that all the airmen listed died in combat.

75 **CROSS IN VILLAGE SQUARE**

Republic Square
Żejtun
Southeast Malta

In various village squares you will find monuments, commemorating personalities or an event. In the small square next to Żejtun Parish church there is a monument with a cross on top of it. This cross was originally located in front of the Capuchin church just outside the fortifications of Cottonera. During the blockade by the Maltese of the French troops, a group of Żejtun men went to this church, retrieving the cross and putting up in the square beneath the fortifications that were held by the French. This was an act of bravado that had nothing to do with the military effort.

76 **GOZO 1551 MONUMENT**
It-Telgħa tal-Belt
Victoria
Gozo

There is a simple monument just outside the Citadel's fortifications, which commemorates the fact that the large majority of the population of Gozo was carried off to slavery during an attack by the Ottoman Empire in 1551. The Ottomans originally landed in Malta, and after realising that the fortifications would take longer to capture than scheduled, they decided to stop in Gozo and besiege the smaller citadel. Unfortunately, after a three-day siege, the population was forced to surrender. While a number of locals had managed to escape by scaling down the walls during the night, the majority ended up being taken captive, ending up in slavery. A dark chapter in Gozitan history.

77 **ASTRONOMICAL CLOCK**
Republic St
Valletta

Besides the various sundials all over the islands, that indicate the time of the day, you can also tell the time in Valletta on the island's only astronomical clock. The first such clock was installed during the second half of the 18th century. The building where it is located was the office of the Treasury of the Knights of Malta, overlooking one of the popular squares of Valletta. The clock, which was restored at the end of the 20th century, indicates the month and horoscope at midday. It is still in good condition.

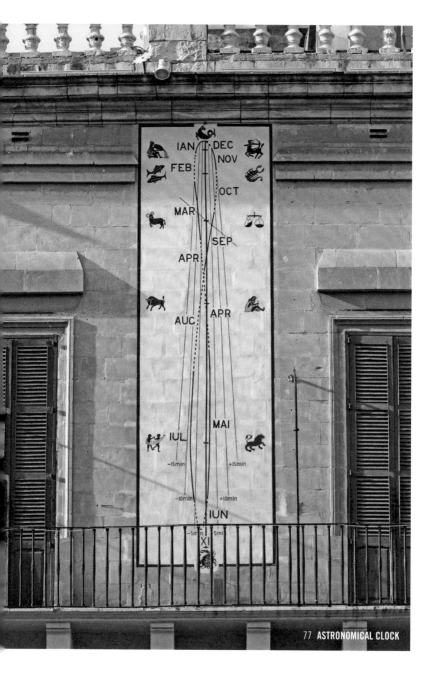

78 **LAFERLA CROSS**

Moghdija tal-Gholja
Siġġiewi
South Malta

A large cross was installed on one of Malta's highest hills at the turn of the 20th century. The original idea was to have a number of statues commemorating the Passion of Christ lining the country path leading up to the top, culminating with the massive cross. A number of stone statues were erected, and the cross was placed on top of a large base. Within the base, there was a small chapel. Unfortunately, the cross had to be replaced more than once due to damage by storms. The view from this hill is quite something – it overlooks the countryside, the terraced fields, the villages below as well as the nearby coastline.

79 **ST PAUL'S STATUE**

St Paul's Island
St Paul's Bay
Northwest Malta

According to the Acts of the Apostles, St Paul was shipwrecked on our islands while on his way to Rome to be tried as a rebel. The location of the spot where his ship was wrecked in a storm is still a mystery, but for many centuries St Paul's Island has traditionally been indicated as the location where this event occurred. Around 1850, a stone statue of St Paul was erected here, placed on a large pedestal, in order to commemorate this important event. In 1990, when St Pope John Paul II visited Malta for the first time, he stopped here while on a sea trip to Gozo and blessed the area.

80 STREET NICHES

Merchants St c/w
Archbishop St
Valletta

The earliest religious niche was installed towards the end of the 17th century in Valletta. Later a German knight came up with the idea of installing statues of saints on the corners of buildings. A candle would be placed in front of these statues, providing street lighting at night. This idea was soon copied and nowadays you can find hundreds of these niches around the Maltese islands, with locals expressing their devotion by installing statues of various sizes and artistic skill on many of street corners. The majority of them are still well kept and taken care of by the locals.

81 TINY CANNON

PALACE ARMOURY
St George's Square
Valletta
+356 2124 9349
heritagemalta.org

One of the greatest collections of armour in Europe can be found in the former Palace of the Grand Masters. The Palace Armoury possesses a number of arms and armour from the late 15th century up to the 18th century, including artillery pieces, some of which are large and very decorative. Others are small and decorated with the coat-of-arms of the donor. The small ones were mainly used on coastal towers. The collection includes a unique light cannon, with part of its barrel made from rope, for easy manoeuvring. An incredible collection, definitely worth a visit.

82 UNDERGROUND MILL

Triq tal-Għajn
Xlendi, Munxar
Gozo
+356 2155 8755
munxar.gov.mt

During the Cold War, the British authorities constructed seven underground flour mills in Malta. The idea was to make sure that bread production would continue in the event of a nuclear attack. While six were constructed in Malta, there was only one in Gozo. These were located deep underground, and they are widely considered an engineering feat. Recently two of these flour mills have been restored, and the one in Gozo is open by appointment through the Local Council.

83 VICTORY MONUMENT

Victory Square
Vittoriosa
Southeast Malta

The first public monument commemorating the Great Siege victory of 1565 dates from 1705. It was installed in the main square of Vittoriosa, the town where most of the hand-to-hand combat and bombardment occurred throughout the summer of 1565. The monument was restored during the 19th century, and the railing that was put up also referenced the conflict between Christians and the Ottoman Muslim troops. The symbols on the railing feature the cross (the symbol of Christianity) defeating the crescent (the symbol of the Muslim troops).

84 WAY OF THE CROSS STATUES

Ta' Pinu St
Gharb
Gozo

Facing the popular and devotional sanctuary of Our Lady of Ta' Pinu, in Gozo there is a hill (Ta' Ghammar), which locals climb while reciting prayers as part of a pilgrimage. Along the unpaved trail there are a number of life-size marble statues that depict the different stages of the Passion of Christ, culminating in the resurrection at the top of the hill. The open arena is used for gatherings. From the top of the hill you have a wonderful view of the surrounding area, including the Citadel.

Forgotten **H I S T O R Y**

85 **FOSSILS**
Triq id-Dwejra
San Lawrenz
Gozo

Malta was formed at the bottom of the then developing Mediterranean Sea. Rivers flowing into the Mediterranean deposited material, forming the limestone layers that make up Malta. At the same time, thousands of sea creatures were also deposited at the bottom of the sea. When you walk around the countryside, you can often spot fossils on exposed rock formations. At Dwejra, there is a large area where fossils of different shapes and sizes can be easily observed. These are the geological records of the formation of the Maltese Islands.

86 **VICTORY KITCHEN SIGN**
Melita St
Valletta

During World War II, Malta was surrounded by enemy territory, making it very difficult for provisions – for the locals and for the military – to arrive on the island. Due to the lack of food supplies in Malta, the British authorities decided to set up a food kitchen. Food was distributed to the people from the Victory Kitchen, and more than 40 such food kitchens were established around Malta. Only one Victory Kitchen sign survives, which was recently discovered while renovating the façade of the building. These kitchens managed to stretch the limited amount of food until provisions arrived in Malta by sea convoy.

Lost **BATTLEFIELDS**

87 **IL-WIDNA**

Triq it-Tarġa
Naxxar
Northwest Malta

This early warning system was installed in Malta in the 1930s. Britain identified five locations where such a sound mirror could be installed, but ultimately only one was built. The idea was to provide advanced warning of any enemy aircraft flying towards Malta from nearby Sicily. The sound mirror was the only one of its kind to be built by the British military authorities outside Britain. It was decommissioned in 1937.

87 IL-WIDNA

88 PROPERTY AND MILESTONE MARKERS

When you walk through the Maltese countryside, you may run into some Lower Coralline Limestone markers. You will notice that some details have been defaced. In the 1840s, the first property markers were installed by the British authorities, with the legend 'VR' for Queen Victoria, or another legend depending on who was the ruling monarch. Later the authorities started putting up oblong stone markers, with the legend '...miles from Valletta'. When World War II broke out, these markers were defaced by the authorities to prevent the enemy from using these markers for information.

89 FORT ST ANGELO

89 FORT ST ANGELO

The Great Siege
of 1565 St
Vittoriosa
Southeast Malta
+356 2540 1800
heritagemalta.org

The origin of Fort St Angelo is lost, but from the Medieval times right up to the Second World War, hostile troops laid siege to it more than once. Its first mention is in documents relating to a naval battle, that occurred just beneath its walls, in the harbour and around the fort in 1283. It is best known, however, for its role during the Great Siege of 1565, when the Ottoman army laid siege to the islands. Fort St Angelo resisted all sea and land attacks. During the Second World War, the fort was the target of more than 60 direct hits during air-raids by the Axis alliance. Today, the Fort is open to the public and a lot of information is provided about the different sieges that it withstood.

90 FORT VERDALA

Alessandra St
Cospicua
Southeast Malta

Construction of Fort Verdala commenced in 1852. It was built between earlier fortifications that had been erected by the Knights of St John. The fort was built to minimise the vacant land between the earlier fortifications. After its decommissioning as a defence, it was converted into a barrack complex. During the two World Wars it was also used as a prisoner of war camp, housing captured German prisoners, including Karl Dönitz, who was to become the Commander in Chief of the German Navy during the Second World War and later succeeded Hitler as the head of state of Nazi Germany.

91 GREAT SIEGE FRESCOES

GRAND MASTER'S
PALACE

St George's Square
Valletta
+356 2124 9349
heritagemalta.org

The Grand Council Chamber of the former Grand Master's Palace is beautifully decorated with a series of frescoes depicting the main events of the Great Siege of 1565. During this siege more than 25,000 Ottoman troops landed in Malta to lay siege to the islands' meagre defences. The small defence force managed to resist all the onslaughts, and although Fort St Elmo was lost, the others were able to soldier on until help arrived from Sicily in early September. The four-month long siege ended with the Ottoman elite troops abandoning the siege and returning home empty-handed. The frescoes illustrate the main battles, the deaths, and the atrocities that were perpetrated during this siege. This is one of the most important elements of visual documentation that we have of the Great Siege.

92 PORTA DEL SOCCORSO

NATIONAL WAR
MUSEUM AND
FORT ST ELMO

Mediterranean St
Valletta
+356 2148 1305
heritagemalta.org

Fort St Elmo is made up of the older Upper Fort and the Lower Fort, which was added during the 18th century. Today the main entrance to the original Fort is referred to as 'Porta del Soccorso', or the gate from where help arrived during the summer of 1565 during the Great Siege. Troops from Fort St Angelo and Vittoriosa managed to enter the besieged fort through this gate and help resist the Ottoman onslaught, thus prolonging the siege. The rebuilt church within the fort is just past the gate. It is here that the Knights made their last stand, before being killed.

93 WORLD WAR II SHELTERS

MALTA AT WAR MUSEUM
Couvre Porte
Vittoriosa
Southeast Malta
+356 2189 6617
maltaatwar
museum.com

During World War II, the Maltese started digging into the ground to create passages and rooms where they could take shelter from the aerial bombardments. Vittoriosa was hard hit, due to its proximity to the harbour. Families that had alternative housing outside the area left the city, while many others went to live in rock-cut shelters. While the larger ones were dug by the authorities, there were individual family shelters as well. The shelters provided the necessary comfort away from the attacks. Entire families lived in the cramped and unhygienic rock-cut rooms, but at least these were deemed to be safe.

PERSONALITIES

to remember

---

94 COMTE DE BEAUJOLAIS

ST JOHN'S
CO-CATHEDRAL

St John's St
Valletta
+356 2122 0536
stjohnsco
cathedral.com

There are four funerary monuments in the Chapel of France, and one of them is dedicated to the memory of Louis Charles, the Comte de Beaujolais and the brother of the future King of France, Louis Philippe I. The young French prince was arrested together with his family. While in prison, he contracted tuberculosis. Eventually he and his brothers were exiled from France and sent to the United States of America. After several adventures, they arrived in England in 1800. Due to Louis Charles's ill health, the brothers travelled to the Mediterranean, stopping in Malta in 1808. A few days later, Louis Charles died. He was buried in St John's Co-Cathedral, while his heart was buried in the small church of Our Lady of Liesse, in Valletta.

95 ST ĠORĠ PRECA

IMMACULATE
CONCEPTION CHURCH

St Joseph High St
Hamrun
South Malta

Born in Valletta, Dun Ġorġ, as he is still affectionally referred to in Malta, became a priest, working with the underprivileged and the illiterate. He established a Religious Society with the aim of teaching Catechism to children, opening up several centres all over the islands. He was honoured by the Pope during his lifetime. In 2007, Dun Ġorġ Preca was canonised by Pope John Paul II. He is buried in a church that he founded, which also serves as the headquarters of the religious society that he established.

96 GAETANO BRUNO

ST JOHN'S
CO-CATHEDRAL
St John's St
Valletta
+356 2122 0536
stjohnsco
cathedral.com

During the turbulent two-year French period in Malta, one of the unsung heroes was Fra Gaetano Bruno, a conventual chaplain of the Order of St John. The French Republican Government tasked him with the supervision of the destruction of various documents and archives held at the Bibliotheca. Bruno succeeded in putting off the job, preserving the important Archives of the Order of St John in the process. Today these archives are used to research the period of the Order of St John while in Malta. Gaetano Bruno is buried in St John's Co-Cathedral, next to Mattia Preti.

97 JUAN B AZOPARDO

Xatt Juan B
Azopardo
Senglea
Southeast Malta

Along the wharf of Senglea, one of the Three Cities, a small marble tablet indicates where Juan B Azopardo was born. He was a privateer, and after having served with various European fleets, he settled in Argentina. He fought in the British invasions of Buenos Aires and later helped to establish the Argentine Navy. Several ships of the Argentine Navy have been named after him, as well as monuments and streets throughout Argentina.

Personalities – **ARTISTS**

98 BILLY CONNOLLY

Malta has always been a big attraction for British retirees, or as a place to have a second home. One of these personalities is Billy Connolly, a Scottish stand-up comedian, singer, and actor. He is best known for his raucous comedy, which has been considered controversial at times.

99 DAVID BOWIE

The young David Bowie travelled to Malta when he was still unknown, taking part in the Malta International Song Festival in 1969. That same year, he also released one of his best-known hits, *Space Oddity*. During his participation in the Malta festival his song was singled out as the best-produced record.

100 JOSEPH CALLEJA

The world famous Maltese-born tenor Joseph Calleja has performed in some of the world's best opera houses. He began singing at the age of 16, making his operating debut at the age of 19 as Macduff in Verdi's *Macbeth*. In 2009, he began a series of annual concerts in Malta, inviting foreign artists to perform with him. During his career he has recorded several albums and videos. In 2013, he starred in the film *The Immigrant* as the tenor Enrico Caruso.

101 **MATTIA PRETI**

An Italian 17th-century painter, Preti was invited to Malta in the 1650s after having been made a Knight of Grace in the Order of St John. After demonstrating his artistic skills, he was invited to paint the whole nave of the Conventual Church of St John in Valletta. He returned to Malta in 1661, spending the remainder of his life on the island, painting a large number of canvases, as well as having a busy bottega. His works are mainly found in Valletta and in several other churches all over the island. Mattia Preti died in 1699 at the age of 86, and he is buried in St John's Co-Cathedral.

100 **JOSEPH CALLEJA**

Personalities – **AUTHORS**

102 **DESMOND MORRIS**

Desmond Morris, a successful author of books, articles and television programmes on animal and human behaviour, settled Malta with his wife. While in Malta he wrote several other books. He famously said that his years in Malta were the happiest of his entire life, and he continued to visit Malta in later years, to film his documentaries.

103 **HANS CHRISTIAN ANDERSEN**

The Danish national poet was in Malta for a day, while travelling from Italy to Greece. During his one day stay he managed to take a tour of the island, on a horse-driven *calesse*, visiting Valletta, Mdina and Rabat as well as other localities. He commented on the arid countryside, as well as the various aspects of places that he visited, the language spoken on Malta and the women's dresses, which he found to be more Oriental than European.

104 NICHOLAS MONSARRAT

A lawyer by profession, Monsarrat enlisted with the Royal Naval Volunteer Reserve when World War II broke out. His adventures with the navy led him to publish his novel *The Cruel Sea* which brought him fame and wealth. He settled in Gozo with his third wife, with the intention to write a novel about Malta during the war. *The Kappillan of Malta* was well received. Although Monsarrat meant to only stay in Malta for a few years, he ended up living in the quiet village of San Lawrenz, Gozo until he died (in London) in 1979.

Personalities – **POLITICIANS**

105 **LORD GERALD STRICKLAND**
UPPER BARRAKKA GARDENS
Valletta

Born in Valletta, he was educated in Malta, England and Italy. He became involved in politics from a young age, and was elected to the Council of the Government of Malta, representing the nobility. After holding various important political positions in Malta and Australia, he returned to Malta soon after the island was granted self-government in 1921. He founded the Anglo-Maltese Party (later called the Constitutional Party) and became the Prime Minister of Malta in 1927. He also founded the *Times of Malta*. There is a monument to Lord Strickland at the Upper Barrakka Gardens, Valletta, and he is buried at the Mdina Cathedral.

105 **LORD GERALD STRICKLAND**

106 NERIK MIZZI

Born in Valletta, Enrico Mizzi (better known as Nerik) studied law in Malta and in Italy. He was the son of the founder of the Nationalist Party, and his involvement in local politics led to conflict with the British administration. During World War I, he was arrested and court-martialled for sedition. In the years between the two World Wars, he held various ministerial positions. In 1940, he was arrested and, together with 47 other Maltese, was deported illegally to Uganda. He was allowed back into the country in 1945. Five years later he became Prime Minister of Malta, only to die three months later. He is commemorated with a monument in front of St John's Co-Cathedral.

107 MARQUIS HASTINGS MONUMENT
HASTING GARDENS
Windmill St
Valletta

In Hastings Gardens, overlooking Marsamxett Harbour, there is a monument to Lord Hastings, one of the first British Governors. An Anglo-Irish politician and military officer, he served as Governor-General of India. After resigning from his role, he was appointed Governor of Malta. He died two years later at sea off Naples. He was buried in Valletta, and according to his wishes, his right hand was cut off to be interred with his wife.

Unusual and strange
MONUMENTS

---

108 CART RUTS

Misraħ Għar il-Kbir
Siġġiewi
South Malta

One of the great mysteries of Maltese archaeology are the many cart ruts that are to be found all over the islands. Some come in pairs, others resemble a busy railway interchange. The group located near Buskett Gardens have been referred to as Clapham Junction, as there are so many of criss-crossing and parallel grooves that the site resembles a train station. At other locations, the ruts seem to run down into the sea. They have not been dated, as no material has ever been discovered that is associated with them. While some archaeologists believe that these cart ruts date from the prehistoric period, others have surmised that they were created in antiquity.

109 DOLMEN

Triq Il-Fortizza
Mosta
Northwest Malta

Dolmens are another type of monument that are found scattered in Malta. These consist of large blocks of stone, elevated from the ground, that rest on smaller stones to form a chamber or tomb. They are believed to be Bronze Age burial chambers. The examples that we have in Malta are of varying sizes.

110 CONGREVE MONUMENT

Ħaġar Qim Road
Qrendi
South Malta

Facing the channel between Malta and the islet of Filfla, there is a monument to commemorate the sea burial of the British Governor, General Sir Walter Norris Congreve. His funeral was held in Valletta, after which his body was transferred to a vessel and he was buried at sea, at the site that he indicated.

110 CONGREVE MONUMENT

111 GRANARIES
THE GRANARIES
Floriana
Southeast Malta

The Granaries are located in one of the large open spaces within the fortifications that surround Valletta and Floriana. Granaries were among the first constructions to be undertaken by the Knights of Saint John within the fortifications, in order to make sure that there would be enough grain in case of a siege. With the increase of British military personnel in Malta, the British authorities saw fit to expand the granaries at Floriana. These granaries were still in use till the 1950s. Nowadays the area is used for large events – whether of a religious, political or cultural nature.

112 MENHIR
St Peter St
Kirkop
South Malta

Menhirs are another type of monument often found in Malta. These upright stones, usually more than two metres tall, feature no decoration whatsoever. Due to the lack of archaeological remains near them, it has been very hard to date these stones, although they are believed to have been created during the last period of Maltese prehistory, namely the Bronze Age.

113 NORMAN COLUMN
Triq Tal-Mużew
Mdina
Northwest Malta

In the garden just outside the fortifications of the medieval city of Mdina, there is a column, surmounted by a cross. Said to date from Norman times, the column could also be a repurposed Roman column. At some point, a cross was added, and the pillar was placed on a number of steps. Apparently it marks the original location of the Augustinian church, which was demolished as it was deemed to be too close to the fortifications of Mdina.

FGURA PARISH CHURCH

BUILDINGS

DETAILS *that make the difference*

---

114 WOODEN BALCONIES
South St
Valletta

The ornate closed wooden balconies on the façades of houses are a typical element of vernacular Maltese architecture. Even large palaces have them, and it is believed that the first ones to be installed in Malta were those of the Grand Master's Palace in Valletta. At the very end of South Street, towards Marsamxett Harbour, you can spot an entire block with these *gallarijas*. These balconies were used to hang clothes while drying, while opening the side windows to allow fresh air to pass through. They are also considered an extension to the house.

115 STONE FIELD HUTS / GIRNA
Mġarr
Northwest Malta

In the northern part of Malta, you will spot several field huts, built from the loose limestone that is found locally. These stone huts, called *girna* in Maltese, have different shapes, and while some may be oval, there are others that are circular, rectangular or squarish. Their size is dictated by the owner's needs. Although they are no longer used by farmers nowadays, in the past these would have served as shelters against bad weather and a place to store one's tools. Their ingenious construction attests to the skills of their builders.

116 FOUNDATION STONE

CHURCH OF OUR
LADY OF VICTORY

South St
Valletta

The laying of the foundation stone of the new city of Valletta was held on 28 March 1566. The ceremony was attended by all the dignitaries of the Order as well as other personalities. Tradition has is that the foundation stone lies where Grand Master Jean de Valette built his own private church, dedicated to Our Lady of Victory. Every year, on the anniversary day, a commemoration is held next to the church, close to a marble tablet that records this event.

115 STONE FIELD HUTS / GIRNA

117 **GRANARIES**

THE GRANARIES
Floriana
Southeast Malta

The Order had dug a number of bell-shaped granaries around the harbour area, in order to have enough grain in case of a siege. During the 19th century, the British authorities added more than 70 similar bell-shaped granaries in front of Floriana Parish Church, given that the number of British military personnel had increased. This meant there would always be enough grain, in case of an enemy attack. Nowadays the open area is used for mass public manifestations, whether religious, political or for entertainment.

117 GRANARIES

118 MTARFA CLOCK TOWER

Triq it-Torri
ta' l-Arloġġ
Mtarfa
Northwest Malta
+356 2145 1145

During the second half of the 19th century, various British military buildings were erected near the hamlet of Mtarfa. Besides barracks and a hospital, a clock tower was also built. The clock tower, which dates from 1895, is an iconic landmark. While the clock has already been restored, the 22,5-metre tower is currently undergoing a facelift, and it will offer spectacular views from the top when it reopens.

119 VEDETTE

GARDJOLA GARDENS
Porto Salvo St
Senglea
Southeast Malta

A characteristic of Maltese fortifications are the various small undecorated towers at strategic locations. The one at Senglea is exceptional in that it is decorated. The decorations around the tower feature an eye and an ear, meaning that the guard must always keep his eyes and ears open, and a crane. A crane holding a stone in its claw is a well-known symbol in heraldry. If the crane falls asleep and lets the rock slip, it will fall on its other claw and wake the crane. This thus implies that a guard must always stay awake, in order to protect the other soldiers.

ICONIC ARCHITECTURE

120 BIBLIOTHECA

36 Old Treasury St
Valletta
+356 2598 3550
maltalibraries.
gov.mt

One of the last buildings to be erected during the 18th century was the Bibliotheca. Designed by Stefano Ittar, this was the first neo-classical building to be built in Malta. Towards the end of the 18th century, the Order realised that it needed a proper depository for the archives and books that it had accumulated since the 16th century. The loss of Malta by the Order to the French troops in 1798 put an end to the transfer of the books to the new building. The Bibliotheca finally welcomed its books and archives in 1812, and it has since retained its importance as a research library. Open to the public.

121 MANOEL THEATRE

Old Theatre St
Valletta
+356 2124 6389
teatrumanoel.
com.mt

Construction on the theatre, which was funded by Grand Master António Manoel de Vilhena, started in 1731 and it was inaugurated one year later. This was the first purposely built theatre in Malta and it is reputed to be Europe's third-oldest working theatre. The theatre fell into disuse, especially during the 19th and early 20th century. It served as a doss house for the homeless, with stalls rented out for the night, and a venue for Carnival balls. The theatre was sold to a private entrepreneur but after World War II, the Maltese Government acquired and restored it. Today it is once again a theatre and a performing arts venue, and you can tour the building. A must for all theatre fans.

122 MEDITERRANEAN CONFERENCE CENTRE

Mediterranean St
Valletta
+356 2124 3840
mcc.com.mt

The building boasts several large halls where meetings, events, and theatre productions are hosted. The original building was built in the 16th century, when Valletta was built. In the 17th century, it was expanded to its present size. Known as the Sacra Infermeria, the Holy Infirmary, it offered the best hospital treatment in the Mediterranean. Patients slept in single beds and were served with silver utensils. After damage during World War II, the building was restored, and converted into a conference centre. Various international conferences and meetings have been held here, including a meeting between President Bush and President Gorbachev in 1989, which ended the Cold War. A must-see.

123 PALAZZO SANTA SOFIA

Villegaignon St
Mdina
Northwest Malta

This is one of the oldest standing buildings in Malta, as a date inscribed on the lintel of a small window indicates. Originally the covered passageway led to an internal courtyard, but it was later opened up as a public street. The pointed archway attests to its medieval origins. Although the upper floor was added in the early 20th century, the addition respected the medieval style and character of the medieval city. There is a typical medieval decoration between the two floors, with the coat of arms of the Santa Sofia noble family on the façade.

124 TA' PINU NATIONAL SHRINE

Triq Ta' Pinu
Gharb
Gozo
+356 2155 6187
tapinu.org

One of the most frequented churches in Gozo is Ta' Pinu National Shrine, which dominates the surrounding countryside, attracting visitors, pilgrims and devotees. The 1920s neo-Romanesque church was built as an extension to the smaller and older church, where a painting of the Assumption of the Blessed Virgin is kept that is said to be miraculous after a spinster called Karmni Grima heard a voice emanating it as she walked past. The church's interior is decorated with excellent stonework, marble and mosaics – very different from the customary decorations of Maltese churches. There is a small and interesting collection of votive offerings by the faithful.

125 SKORBA PREHISTORIC SITE

Triq l-Imqades
Mġarr
Northwest Malta
+356 2158 0590
heritagemalta.org

The first humans to settle in Malta lived either in caves, or in open air villages. The earliest village is located at Skorba, on the outskirts of Mġarr, and is still surrounded by good arable land. This dates from around 6000 BC. The site continued to be used for habitation purposes, and around 3500 BC a temple was erected here. Interesting finds were unearthed here, including the earliest human representation from prehistoric Malta. When you visit this multi-layered site, you will understand why it has been added to the UNESCO World Heritage List.

126 TA' HAĠRAT PREHISTORIC TEMPLE

St Peter St
Mġarr
Northwest Malta
+356 2158 6264
heritagemalta.org

Like many other prehistoric sites, this is a multi-layered one, with the earliest inhabitants erecting small huts on the site and, after honing their building techniques, constructing one of the most impressive prehistoric temples of Malta in the same location. The monumental façade is impressive, and it is one of only a handful with steps in front of the entrance. An impressive small model of a prehistoric building was found here, which is now exhibited at the National Museum of Archaeology in Valletta. Another prehistoric site that has been recognised as UNESCO World Heritage Site.

Formidable **FORTIFICATIONS**

127 **COTTONERA GATE**

FODNAZZJONI
WIRT ARTNA
Triq il-Kottonera
Vittoriosa
Southeast Malta
+356 2180 0992
wirtartna.org

In 1670, construction started on a new line of fortifications, to be called the Cottonera Lines, as they were commissioned by Grand Master Nicolás Cotoner. The whole line of defence had several ornamental baroque gates, the main one being Żabbar Gate, or Our Lady of Graces Gate. The gate is both impressive in size and decoration. Recently restored, it is now used by an NGO called Fondazzjoni Wirt Artna, which works to preserve local military heritage. The Grand Master's bust sits at the top of the gate.

128 **DWEJRA TOWER**

Triq id-Dwejra
San Lawrenz
Gozo
+356 2122 0358
dinlarthelwa.org

The 17th century saw an increase in the erection of coastal fortifications around the islands, of which several have been preserved. One of these can be found at Dwejra, on the Gozitan coast, and was built in 1652. The tower's design was meant to offer shelter to the coastguards and token resistance in the event that a small landing force tried to come ashore. Each tower had two single room floors, and guards would enter from the second floor. Originally the tower had a wooden drawbridge. Dwejra Tower also has a stone staircase. Today it is in good condition and open to the public.

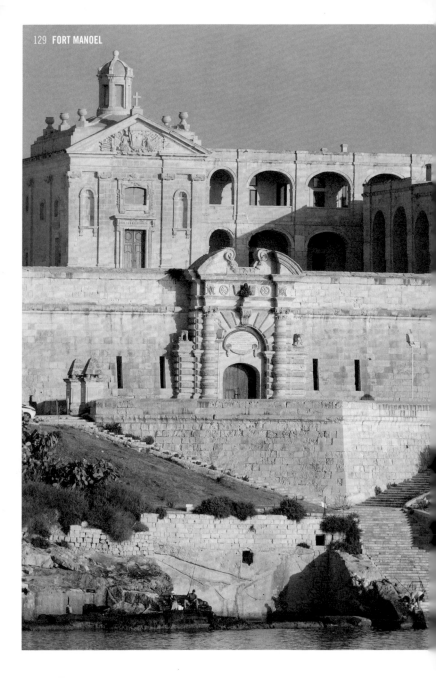

129 FORT MANOEL

Manoel Island
Gżira
Central Malta
+356 2065 5500
midimalta.com

One of the forts built by the Knights of St John in the 18th century, during the reign of Grand Master António Manoel de Vilhena. One of the best completed fortifications, it was later used by the British authorities. During World War II it was a submarine base, suffering a number of direct hits. After years of abandonment, it has recently been restored, and in recent years a number of open days have been organised. The fort offers visitors a closer look at military architecture and excellent views of Marsamxett Harbour and Valletta.

130 FOUGASSE

Xatt L-Aħmar
Għajnsielem
Gozo

The fougasse was an ingenious way to add more firepower to the defence of the coastline. These large well-like holes were dug at a 45-degree angle into the rock, close to the shoreline. Gunpowder would be placed at the bottom of the hole, topped with several stone boulders of varying dimensions. Essentially the hollow was shaped to simulate a mortar and fire these boulders at the unsuspecting enemy. These fougasses were introduced in Malta in 1740 and more than 60 have since been excavated along the coastline of the islands. This is one of the best preserved.

131 IT-TOQBA SALLY PORT

Triq il-Miratur
Vittoriosa
Southeast Malta

Fortifications needed to have small, narrow and hidden entrances, away from the main land front, for help to enter or even for messengers to leave unseen. A sally port was also used for sorties against the enemy lines. These entries in the fortifications would be well hidden, just like here. The It-Toqba sally port leads to the shoreline, from where you could continue your journey without being spotted. During the Great Siege of 1565, messengers and even help passed through this small doorway.

132 SALUTING BATTERY AND LASCARIS WAR ROOMS

UPPER BARRAKKA
GARDENS
Valletta
+356 2180 0992
lascariswar
rooms.com

Besides enjoying the magnificent view of the Grand Harbour and the surrounding fortifications from Valletta's ramparts, you can also attend the firing of the gun salute twice a day from the saluting battery in the Upper Barrakka Gardens. Re-enactors portraying the late 19th-century British Army man the site. You can also visit the Lascaris War Rooms here, from where the island's defence was supervised during World War II. Learn more about Malta's role during the hostilities, the communications used and the planning of the invasion of Sicily.

133 RED TOWER

Triq Tad-Dahar
Mellieħa
Northwest Malta
+356 2122 0358
dinlarthelwa.org

The north of the island was still largely undefended in the middle of the 17th century. Various small watch towers were subsequently built, but this tower was much larger as this end of the island was deemed too vulnerable to enemy landings. Called St Agatha's Tower, but known as the Red Tower, it served as a communication tower between Gozo and Malta. Built in 1649, the tower had four bastioned corners with room for five cannons on the roof. During the 18th century low lying defence walls were added to provide a defensive location for troops stationed in the Mellieħa Bay area. Today it is managed by an NGO called Din L-Art Ħelwa and is open to the public.

132 SALUTING BATTERY AND LASCARIS WAR ROOMS

134 ST MARY'S TOWER

Comino
+356 2122 0358
dinlarthelwa.org

This was the sixth coastal tower built by Grand Master Alof de Wignacourt. Erected in 1618, this large bastioned watchtower provided the island of Comino with a defence as ships travelling the straits between Malta and Gozo were often attacked by corsairs. Built on a large platform, the guards in the tower would have had an excellent view of the surrounding landscape and sea. Although not used in the defence of Malta during the invasion by the French in 1798, it later served as a prison for French sympathisers during that same period. Today it is managed by an NGO called Din L-Art Ħelwa and is open to the public.

135 VICTORIA LINES

Binġemma Road
Rabat
Northwest Malta

This is a 12-kilometre-long line of fortifications along the North West front. Built during the second half of the 19th century by the British authorities, in order to offer better protection to the Grand Harbour areas where the British Navy had its headquarters, this entrenchment was strengthened with forts and batteries along the route. A walk along these Lines offers excellent views of the surrounding coastline and countryside. The Lines cross over valleys and follow the contours of the landscape. Originally called the North West Front, they were later renamed the Victoria Lines to commemorate Queen Victoria's Diamond Jubilee.

Inspiring NEW ARCHITECTURE

136 FGURA PARISH CHURCH

Hompesch Road
Fgura
Southeast Malta
+356 2180 2992
fguraparish.org

This is one of the most modern churches to be recently built in Malta. The architect made use of reinforced concrete, and the design is different from the usual Latin cross form that is so widely used in Christian churches. It provides ample space inside, but rather than a long nave, it has a tent-like structure over the whole interior. Although the façade is interesting to look at, it is better appreciated from above.

137 MILLENNIUM CHAPEL

Church St
Paceville
Central Malta
+356 2135 4464
millennium chapel.org

Following the modern development of a once idyllic summer village, Paceville, into a modern vibrant and tourist resort, a church was built to cater to the growing population. The modern structure differs from the baroque churches of the past. The roof of the semi-circular structure is supported by a number of pillars. In recent years, another religious space was erected next to the main church, called the Millennium Chapel. This oasis of peace takes a different approach to the spiritual space, in the form of an intimate and minimalist building.

138 PARLIAMENT HOUSE

Republic St
Valletta
+356 2559 6000
parliament.mt

Upon entering the walled 16th-century city of Valletta, the first building that you see is the 21st-century Parliament House, a design of the famous Italian architect Renzo Piano. The building consists of two blocks, placed on stilts, and connected with bridges. Each block has three floors; one houses the Chamber where Parliament sessions are held, while the other block is used for the various offices. It is one of the most modern structures to have been erected in Malta, and a zero emission building. The cladding of the façade was made to look like it has been weathered naturally.

139 ST FRANCIS OF ASSISI CHURCH

Tourist St
Qawra
Northwest Malta
+356 2157 7088
qawrachurch.com

Built to a design of the Maltese architect Richard England, this modern church is a landmark among the rest of the surrounding, more tourist-oriented architecture. The church is made up of various geometric designs – columns, triangles, perforated screens, freestanding walls and a round core structure, all contributing to creating a different kind of a sacred place. The interior is designed to allow the faithful to engage directly with the main altar.

140 ST THERESE OF LISIEUX SANCTUARY

Triq il-Wied
Birkirkara
Central Malta
+356 2144 5356

Built after Vatican Council II, this church has a modern rotunda-style structure. The innovative style is also complimented by the use of reinforced concrete and a folded roof structure. The rough stone was left unfinished. Next to it is a 40-metre bell tower.

Architectural **ODDITIES**

141 CALENDAR IN STONE

HAĠAR QIM AND
MNAJDRA PREHISTORIC
TEMPLES
Triq Ħaġar Qim
Qrendi
South Malta
+356 2142 4231
heritagemalta.org

One of the most important prehistoric megalithic monuments still standing in Malta is the Mnajdra complex of three temples. The southern temple is unique, as it is astronomically aligned and was built to indicate the change in seasons. Sunrise is clearly the focal point of this stone calendar, as the first rays of sunlight during the solstice light up decorated upright stones blocks or megaliths in the doorways. During the equinox, the light passes straight through the building to reach the innermost niche. These buildings are among the most ancient religious sites on earth, dating from the fourth millennium BC and are on the UNESCO World Heritage List.

142 NAPOLEON'S STAY

PALAZZO PARISIO
Merchants St
Valletta

In June 1798, Napoleon Bonaparte stopped in Malta on his way to Egypt, captured the islands, taking over from the Knights of the Order of St John. During his brief stay in Malta, he resided at the then privately owned Palazzo Parisio, from where he issued a number of controversial orders. Today the building is used by the Ministry for Foreign Affairs.

Palatial **DWELLINGS**

143 **CASA ROCCA PICCOLA**

74 Republic St
Valletta
+356 2122 1499
*casarocca
piccola.com*

This privately owned family home belongs to a noble family. The original building dates from the second half of the 16th century, when it was the residence of one of the Admirals of the Order of St John, Don Pietro La Rocca. It was later occupied by various knights, after which it passed into the hands of a Maltese aristocratic family. Casa Rocca Piccola houses a number of rooms and halls, that are richly decorated with family heirlooms, a library with ancient and precious documents, as well as authentic furniture and other household items. Beneath the house is a World War II shelter, to which the inhabitants withdrew for safety during the many air raids.

144 **GIRGENTI PALACE**

Limiti Tal-Għajn
il-Kbira
Siġġiewi
South Malta

The Inquisitors built their summer residence here in this lush valley and the surrounding countryside in the late 17th century. The building was a functional small residence for the representative of the Pope in Malta. A small church was erected nearby, that connected with the Palace through a covered passageway. Today it is the official summer residence of the Prime Minister of Malta.

145 SAN ANTON PALACE

Birbal St
Attard
Central Malta
president.gov.mt/
sant-anton-palace

The private residence of the future Grand Master Antoine de Paule, this country retreat soon became the favourite residence of the Grand Masters. Surrounded by lush gardens, part of which have been opened to the public, it is still a popular place with locals. The palace, which is surrounded by private gardens, is not open to the public, as it is the official residence of the President of Malta. Although the interior is opulently decorated, the exterior looks more austere.

145 SAN ANTON PALACE

146 **PALAZZO FALSON**

Villegaignon St
Mdina
Northwest Malta
+356 2145 4512
palazzofalson.com

The earliest part of this palace dates from the 13th century, and it is believed that a medieval synagogue existed on the site. Various alterations and additions were made during the following centuries. The house changed hands and was eventually purchased by Olof Gollcher, an avid collector of *objets d'art*, ranging from Persian carpets, armour, furniture and paintings. The various rooms of this medieval building make it a unique place to visit. The house was restored by the Fondazzjoni Patrimonju Malti and opened to the public in 2007.

147 **PALAZZO PARISIO SUMMER RESIDENCE**

Victory Square
Naxxar
Northwest Malta
+356 2141 2461
palazzoparisio.com

In 1898, a wealthy Maltese banker, philanthropist and merchant named Marquis Giuseppe Scicluna bought this small 18th-century country retreat, turning it into a magnificent and richly decorated residence. No expense was spared in the embellishment of his new residence, with sweeping marble staircases, moulded ceilings and crystal chandeliers making it one of the most opulent homes in Malta. The various rooms are still decorated with the original furniture, while the large, recently restored banqueting hall shows the lengths to which the Marquis went in his love for design. The palace is open to the public and is used to host corporate events.

148 VERDALA PALACE

Buskett Road
Rabat
Northwest Malta

Built towards the end of the 16th century as a retreat by Grand Master Verdalle, Verdala Palace soon became a favourite summer residence of the Grand Masters and Knights in the following centuries. The palace was used to receive important visitors, and lavish banquets for distinguished visitors were also held here. It was also a hunting lodge, giving its setting in a woodland area. The building resembles a fortified countryside villa, surrounded by a stone quarried ditch, with a small church nearby. Formerly used by the British Governors, since 1974, the palace has been used as the summer residence of the President of Malta.

149 VILLA BOLOGNA

St Anthony St
Attard
Central Malta
+356 9953 7925
villabologna.com

Built in the 18th century as a wedding gift to the daughter of the advisor of Grand Master Emmanuel Pinto de Fonseca, the house was considered one of the most beautiful palaces of its time. The villa has lush gardens, that accentuate the building's beauty. Currently held by Lord Strickland, a former Prime Minister of Malta, the villa has recently been restored and opened to the public.

MEDIEVAL MDINA

PLACES

ENIGMATIC PLACES

150 ST AGATHA'S CATACOMBS

St Agatha St
Hal Bajjada
Rabat
Northwest Malta
+356 2145 4503
stagathamalta.com

One of several underground cemeteries, better known as Catacombs, with tombs that date to the 3nd and 4rd century AD while the rock church dates from the Middle Ages. Some of the catacombs are decorated, with some of the earliest paintings to be found in Malta. The cave church features several rock paintings, representing different saints. Saint Agatha is said to have taken refuge in this cave after leaving nearby Catania to escape Roman persecution. Unfortunately, she later returned and was martyred. St Agatha is one of the minor patron saints of Malta.

151 SEASIDE BATHS

Marina St
Kalkara
Southeast Malta

The Old British Royal Navy Hospital, dating from the 1830s, once stood on one of the headlands in the Grand Harbour where Esplora is located today. A number of stone structures still remain, such as the shore baths which were used for special medical treatment and the water lift, which was used to bring patients up to the hospital from the shoreline.

152 GHAR IL-KBIR

Triq Inzul ix-Xemx
Siġġiewi
South Malta

The largest and best-known cave complex. In medieval times, a large community occupied the caves, rearing animals, selling their products in the nearby villages, and mainly keeping to themselves. Even during the Great Siege of 1565, they refused to retreat to the safety of Mdina. When they were discovered by the Ottoman troops, they were forced to seek shelter within the city. The community was visited by various foreign visitors to Malta, as it was considered so different from the rest of the islands. In the 1830s the British authorities decided that people living in caves were a health hazard, leading to their eviction. After some of the cave dwellers returned, the authorities destroyed parts of the complex to prevent them from doing so. There are other smaller caves nearby as well as Punic tombs and the mysterious cart ruts.

153 ROYAL OPERA HOUSE RUINS

PJAZZA TEATRU RJAL
Republic St
Valletta
+356 2247 8100
culture.gov.mt/en/
pjazzateatrurjal

Upon entering Valletta through the main gate, next to the new Parliament House, you may notice an open-air theatre. The building is a mix of the foundations of the old 19th-century Royal Opera House and a modern addition by Renzo Piano. The original theatre was constructed during the second half of the 19th century. Although there were problems with the building, and it was even partly destroyed after an accidental fire, the theatre thrived until it was severely damaged during a WWII air raid. Despite several intentions to restore the theatre to its former glory, nothing came of it. In 2013, the remaining ruined structure was finally given a new lease of life as an open-air performance venue.

154 ST PAUL'S GROTTO

WIGNACOURT MUSEUM
College St
Rabat
Northwest Malta
+356 2749 4905
wignacourt
museum.com

The Wignacourt Museum complex features various exhibition halls, a Second World War shelter and other items of interest, but its showpiece is St Paul's Grotto. Saint Paul is said to have stayed here after being shipwrecked on the island in 60 AD, while on his way to Rome from Crete. He is thought to have introduced Christianity to Malta from this site, which is why it is such a venerated place. Many personalities have visited the place, included the last three Popes. Underground altars have been erected around the cave as well as a church, with a college of chaplains who take care of the grotto and promote the devotion of Saint Paul. Today, the grotto is part of a well-designed museum.

155 TAL-VIRTU PALACE

Triq Tal-Virtu
Rabat
Northwest Malta

An architectural folly, built in the shape of a turreted building, on a hilltop. It dominates the skyline, and although it is private property, you can still admire the building's eclectic architecture.

156 BIRKIRKARA OLD RAILWAY STATION AND GARDEN

Triq Salvu Psaila
Birkirkara
Central Malta

A railway used to connect Valletta and Mdina, the old capital city. The main station in between these two locations was located at Birkirkara, at the halfway stage. Following the introduction of modern transport, which was cheaper with more frequent stops, the train service was abolished in 1931. There are very few remnants of this first type of mass transport in Malta, but Birkirkara Station is still standing. It is currently being restored to house a museum dedicated to Malta's railway. The building features some interesting details, and you can see one of the train carriages nearby.

HIDDEN FILM *sets*

157 **CAPTAIN PHILLIPS**

MALTA FILM STUDIOS
St Rocco St
Kalkara
Southeast Malta
+356 2180 9135
*maltafilmstudios.
com.mt*

In 2013, *Captain Phillips* was filmed on location in Malta, starring Tom Hanks among others. The crew shot on three locations, namely the open sea, Malta Freeport and the Malta Film Studios. The film studios boast an indoor water tank, which is of great help when filming open sea scenes, in the safety of an enclosed area.

158 **THE DA VINCI CODE**

Couvre Porte
Vittoriosa
Southeast Malta

A few of the scenes of the blockbuster *The Da Vince Code* were shot in Malta. Some did not make the final cut, but others, such as the scene of Mary Magdalene fleeing from Jerusalem did. This scene was filmed on the bridge within the old entrance of Vittoriosa. Another Tom Hanks vehicle.

159 **GAME OF THRONES**

Mdina
Northwest Malta

Many of the scenes in Season 1 of this popular series were shot in Malta. Mdina, the old capital city, was one of the main sites. The main entrance to the city, the narrow streets, the courtyards and small public squares are easily recognisable for aficionados of the *Game of Thrones*. Walk the streets of Mdina to relive Season 1.

160 GLADIATOR

FORT RICASOLI
St Rocco St
Kalkara
Southeast Malta

Another blockbuster, with an enchanting soundtrack, with more than 45% of the scenes filmed in Malta. The film set at Fort Ricasoli was built to look like the Colosseum, Roman buildings and other such sets, while other sites were used for specific scenes. The crew spent more than 19 weeks filming in Malta. Oliver Reed, one of the lead actors, died while drinking at a local pub.

161 MIDNIGHT EXPRESS

Fort St Elmo
Valletta

A great local's favourite, with many locals starring as extras. The film recounts the story of a young American who is sent to prison in Turkey for trying to smuggle drugs. The story focuses on his time in prison and the living hell that he had to go through to survive, until finally he manages to escape. A powerful film, directed by Alan Parker, with a memorable soundtrack.

162 MUNICH

Dock No 1
Cospicua
Southeast Malta

Directed by Steven Spielberg, more than 90% of this historical drama was shot in Malta on various locations. The film is based on the revenge of the Israeli Government against the terrorists that killed Israeli athletes at the 1972 Munich Olympics. Apparently, the crew filmed at more than 40 different locations across Malta, with sites standing in for other European and Middle Eastern cities.

163 PIRATES

Mdina
Northwest Malta

An adventure comedy film directed by Roman Polanski that was filmed in Mdina, the medieval capital city of Malta, a city which must have seen its fair share of sea pirates/corsairs throughout its millennial history. The typical medieval streets only needed camouflaging with some laundry and other simple things to make them look more authentic.

164 POPEYE VILLAGE

Anchor Bay
Triq il-Prajjiet
Mellieha
Northwest Malta
+356 2152 4782
popeyemalta.com

A film directed by Robert Altman and starring Robin Williams as Popeye provided Malta with an abandoned film set. The entire film was shot in Malta, and a whole village, consisting of 19 buildings, was built along the shores of a small bay. This was one of the first big screen roles for Robin Williams. During one of the scenes, he sustained a head injury requiring stitches and delaying the filming by a number of weeks. You can still visit the film set today.

165 SWEPT AWAY

Comino

Directed by Guy Ritchie and starring Madonna, his wife at the time, the film was shot in various locations in Malta. The snorkelling scenes with Madonna were filmed on Comino. Because Madonna staying in Malta with two of her children, she needed security. Unfortunately, the film failed on box office.

166 THE COUNT OF MONTE CRISTO
ST MARY'S TOWER
Comino

Based on the well-known story by Alexander Dumas, the film was shot in Malta in various locations. The castle on Comino was used as the Chateau d'If, while the Vittoriosa Marina and Mdina were featured in other scenes.

167 TROY
Għajn Tuffieħa /
Golden Bay
Mġarr
Northwest Malta

Brad Pitt and Orlando Bloom travelled to Malta to film this blockbuster. The main sets representing *Troy* were built within Fort Ricasoli, as it is the fort with the largest open area. Other scenes were filmed all over the islands, and at the Malta Film Studios. The sandy bays of Għajn Tuffieħa and Golden Bay were cordoned off to film several scenes.

168 WORLD WAR Z
Republic St
Valletta

Brad Pitt returned to Malta to star in this apocalyptic film with large crowds, that were made up of local extras. Besides the narrow streets at the lower end of Valletta, scenes were also shot at other locations, namely Għajn Tuffieħa and the old ship terminal in Marsa.

Lost **L A N E S**

169 **MEDIEVAL MDINA**
Gatto Murina St
and Mesquita
Square
Mdina
Northwest Malta

A visit to Mdina is always full of surprises. The main streets with their baroque buildings are impressive. But there is also another part of Mdina, with narrow lanes and streets that are dominated by the elegant façades of buildings, that used to be owned by Malta's nobility at one time. The street names and the Middle Age architecture are part of the fascination of medieval Mdina.

170 **TRIQ IL-KBIRA**
Ħaż-Żebbuġ
South Malta

At the entrance to this large town, there is a late 18th-century arch to commemorate when the village was made a city by the then Grand Master, Emanuel de Rohan. The village's former main street lies behind the arch. It leads through the heart of the town, past large mansions, other humbler dwellings, small churches and street decorations, to the parish church. This section gives you a fairly good idea of the layout of the old village, around a street, with other smaller and narrower streets leading to other mysterious and interesting neighbourhoods.

171 LANES AND NARROW STREETS

North St
Vittoriosa
Southeast Malta

So many villages still have authentic narrow streets and lanes. As you walk through the historical centre of Vittoriosa, it is easy to get lost in the narrow streets, and still feel surrounded by history. The narrow streets are often lined with wonderful buildings, large palaces, and even small residences for the locals, that are well-kept, leaving you to wonder about the mysteries that lie behind their doors.

172 TRIQ IL-KARITA AND TRIQ ID-DEJQA

Victoria
Gozo

Just off the small main square of Victoria is another smaller square, opposite the basilica of St George. Besides visiting the church, take a walk through the narrow streets in the area. To your left, there is the small, exquisite Il-Hagar Gozo museum. Explore the winding narrow streets as well as the side lanes and streets, which hold plenty of surprises. One of the most authentic areas of old Victoria.

173 STRAIT STREET

Valletta

Running the entire length of the city of Valletta, this street was originally intended to be narrow. It was meant to separate parts of the city, but it eventually became well-known for being the place where illegal sword fights were organised by the Knights of Malta. During the 19th and 20th centuries, part of this street became popular with British servicemen, as this was where a number of bars, restaurants and dance halls were located. This also explains its unsavoury reputation. In recent years, these same premises have been turned into upmarket restaurants and bars.

BIRGUFEST

EXPERIENCES ⚡

Top **ANNUAL EVENTS**
in Malta

174 MDINA MEDIEVAL FESTIVAL

VARIOUS LOCATIONS
Mdina
Northwest Malta
+356 2145 0707
medievalmdina.eu

Historical re-enactments have become synonymous with the medieval city of Mdina. Once a year the streets once again serve as a backdrop that evokes Malta's late medieval backdrop, with historical re-enactors, shows and even medieval music performed throughout the weekend. A fun event and a unique opportunity to travel back into time.

175 NOTTE BIANCA

Republic St
Valletta
+356 2334 7201
artscouncilmalta.org

An annual event in October when people take to the streets of Valletta to celebrate the arts and culture – with cultural walks, and buildings that are usually closed to the public open to visitors, museums and other cultural places that are open for free, and a motley crew of musical performers providing entertainment on the streets and squares of the capital city. Valletta as never seen before.

176 VALLETTA BAROQUE FESTIVAL

MANOEL THEATRE
Old Theatre St
Valletta
+356 2124 6389
teatrumanoel.com.mt

During the month of January, a number of musical events are organised at the 18th-century Manoel Theatre, and in other venues around the islands. All the venues date from the baroque period, whereas the music covers a wide spectrum of eras and periods. This festival traditionally brings well-known local and international musical performers to the islands, with performances also including lesser-known compositions.

177 BIRGUFEST

Triq il-Majjistral
Vittoriosa
Southeast Malta
+356 2166 2166
birgu.lc@gov.mt

An annual event organised by the local council, featuring a weekend of cultural and festive activities. The main attraction is when all the public lights are switched off for the night, and the streets are lit with thousands of tiny red candles. Various events take place, with historical re-enactors wearing costumes of centuries past and giving the public a glimpse of what life might have looked like in the past. Many of the city's museums also host themed evening activities.

175 **NOTTE BIANCA**

TRADITIONS *and* CUSTOMS
only the Maltese would understand

---

178 BOĊĊI
Triq il-Kunvent
Żabbar
Southeast Malta

The word *boċċi* means marbles, but in Malta this refers to an old street game that is played with wooden balls in various sizes. This is a game for all seasons, and there is also a national league with different village clubs. In summer *boċċi* is a popular pastime, to be played with neighbours, usually in the evening and mostly near the sea. There are a number of courts all around the islands, where you can see people practicing and playing this game.

180 FESTA FIREWORKS

179 FESTA

St Lawrence St
Vittoriosa
Southeast Malta

The Maltese *festa* or village feast is the main event of the year in many communities. More than just a religious procession, these local feasts are a celebration and demonstration of pride, with villagers lavishly decorating their church and streets and organising various festive events throughout the feast week. It is also an opportunity to visit the churches, as many cultural treasures are usually on display. The Feast of St Lawrence is celebrated on the 10th of August, with the city decked out with banners, flags and other street decorations. A must-see.

180 FESTA FIREWORKS

Triq il-Konvoy
ta' Santa Marija
Mqabba
South Malta

No Maltese feast is complete without a proper fireworks display. They usually start one week before the feast day and continue to increase in volume and output throughout the week, with the main event taking place on the eve of the feast day. This is held late in the evening so everyone can enjoy the colourful display. The fireworks at Mqabba are particularly impressive.

181 FESTA STREET DECORATIONS

Republic St
Valletta

Each parish puts up excellent and decorative street ornaments for its feast week, such as heavy damask banners that are richly decorated with floral designs or even paintings of saints. There will be lots of flags flying from the rooftops, offering a unique spectacle. The street decorations usually also include life-size papier mâché statues of saints associated with the patron saint, that are placed on wooden pedestals. These have been painted to look like marble. The main decorations would be near the church. Definitely worth checking out.

182 MNARJA FOLK FESTIVAL

BUSKETT GARDENS
Siġġiewi
South Malta

A traditional summer feast that has its origins in rural communities, where they celebrated summer and a good harvest. The feast is held in a woodland area called Buskett Gardens where the activities kick off on the eve of the 29th June. During the evening and throughout the night, people have a good time, eating the traditional rabbit stew and washing it down with local wine while singing folk tunes. The following day, a public holiday, there is an agricultural show and competition, with bareback horse races in the afternoon. A typical agricultural feast.

183 STATUE BEARERS

The main attraction of any religious feast is a large statue of the patron saint, borne on the shoulders of eight or ten strong men. The statue is usually lavishly decorated, and heavy as well. The islanders sometimes fight for the honour to be one of the statue bearers and in one of the villages there is even an auction to determine who may carry the statue. The proceeds are usually donated to charity. In some towns, the title of statue bearer is handed down from father to son. It takes a lot of dedication and devotion to be a statue bearer.

184 OUR LADY OF LIESSE RELIGIOUS FEAST

Triq Liesse
Valletta

The feast day of Our Lady of Liesse is a smaller feast compared to the ones organised by the main parishes. But it still tends to attract a huge crowd due to its more traditional activities and the beautiful setting on the shores of the Grand Harbour. Some years the feast coincides with an international fireworks festival, also held in the same Grand Harbour, which adds a nice touch. Do visit the lavishly decorated church.

185 ST PHILIP'S BAND CLUB

12 Misraħ San Filep
Ħaż-Żebbuġ
South Malta
+356 2744 4234
bandasanfilep.com.mt

Brass bands are an integral part of the many religious and public festas that are held in each village and parish, with local musicians organising themselves in a band club. These band clubs are more than a social club, as they play an essential role in the outdoor festivities that take place in honour of the patron saint. Visit the club premises during the feast day, when they are beautifully decorated and proudly display their honours.

Unexpected **V I E W S**

186 TA' GIORDAN LIGHTHOUSE

Triq il-Lanterna
Għasri
Gozo

One of the smaller villages of Gozo is set in the countryside, making it a great location for country walks. From the square in front of the parish church, take the road to Tal-Fanal, walk along the country lane and climb up the hill. From the outcrop, you can see the northern most coastline of Gozo and the surrounding countryside. A truly unforgettable view. The lighthouse is still in use, with the present structure dating from 1853.

187 TA' KENUNA TOWER

TA' KENUNA
BOTANICAL GARDEN
Archbishop Saver
Cassar St
Nadur
Gozo

A favourite stop that commands a good view of the surrounding area, the villages below, and the channel between the islands of Gozo, Comino and Malta. A 19th-century telegraphic tower, that was recently restored, stands on top of the hill. This is one of those places where you can spend some time admiring the surrounding area, with 360-degree views of Gozo.

187 VIEW FROM TA' KENUNA TOWER

188 WARDIJA TA' SAN ĠORĠ

Triq Panoramika
Dingli
Northwest Malta

Stop to admire the excellent location of the Bronze Age site, which is situated in a very defensive position. The surrounding cliffs are amongst the highest in Malta. You can walk down the rough path that is located to one side of the archaeological site, leading to the small hamlet of Fawwara. Check out the baroque church and the various cave openings in the cliff face, which until recently were still inhabited.

189 SALINA NATURE RESERVE

Salina Coast Road
Naxxar
Northwest Malta
+356 2143 3265
birdlifemalta.org

This reserve lies in what used to be the inner part of a harbour, but due to large salt deposits, it has become a saline marshland, where a number of salt pans were built in the 16th century. The three large timber huts, originally built in the 18th century, have been restored a number of times and are used to store the salt. Recently, a project was developed within a protected area with the aim of attracting migrating birds on their trek between Africa and Europe. The reserve is open to the public so you can observe birdlife from a distance.

190 SALT PANS

Triq ix-Xwejni
Żebbuġ
Gozo

Salt pans are inextricably linked with the Mediterranean, and there are several along Malta's coastline. Salt is still harvested on Gozo, including along the shore at Qbajjar, where there are several salt pans, stretching for over a kilometre. The pans are filled with sea water, and after the sun evaporates the water, the salt is harvested manually. The salt is usually sold at the local markets and is considered the best, in particular for cooking fish.

Unique CITY TOURS

191 CITADEL AND VICTORIA
START AT:
MISRAH IT-TOKK
Victoria
Gozo

Start your walk from the medieval part of Victoria, climbing up the steep hill to the Citadel. While the narrow and winding streets of Victoria have a mesmerising atmosphere, as you walk past narrow streets, passages and churches, the walk up to the Citadel offers a completely different experience. Both towns have churches and museums you can visit. The Citadel is surrounded by medieval and 16th-century fortifications, overlooked by the 17th-century baroque Cathedral of the Assumption.

192 GHASRI – GHARB – SAN LAWRENZ
Pjazza s-Salvatur
Għasri
Gozo

Start your walk at the parish church of Għasri, one of the smallest villages on the Maltese Islands. As you walk along the road, which is not that busy, you will spot old farmhouses, some of which have been converted into tourist accommodation, and the popular and devotional church known as Our Lady of Ta' Pinu, which leads towards the village of Għarb. Take the street downhill towards the countryside, until you reach the next village of San Lawrenz. A country walk, with plenty of fresh air, peace and quiet, and an opportunity to see some interesting churches and rural architecture.

193 NAXXAR

Triq il-Markiz
Giuseppe Scicluna
Naxxar
Northwest Malta

The town of Naxxar is an interesting mix of old medieval streets and lanes, surrounded by modern buildings and more recent development. The church at the centre of the town is imposing. There is a private and very richly decorated palace nearby called Palazzo Parisio. Take a stroll down the narrow streets behind the palace to admire the city's vernacular architecture and typical small churches.

194 RABAT AND MDINA

Is-Saqqajja
Rabat
Northwest Malta

Mdina, the old capital city of Malta, and its suburb of Rabat offer medieval architecture, historic centres, imposing churches and other smaller religious sites, as well as some of the best museums on the islands. The impact of the 1693 earthquake is more palpable in Mdina, with its older buildings that survived and the rebuilt area which dates from the 18th century. Both towns have winding and narrow streets, with picturesque dead-end streets and quiet alleys that photographers will love.

195 THREE VILLAGES

Triq Birbal
Attard
Central Malta

Nowadays the original three small villages – Attard, Balzan and Lija – are surrounded by recent developments. But the centres of each of these villages have been preserved, with so many characteristics of village life. Here the nobility and the well-to-do built their country residences. They are easy to recognise, with their large façades, their beautiful, ornate architecture, and their spacious gardens. The smaller buildings have their own particular details which make a walk in this area a unique experience.

196 THE THREE CITIES

Triq il-Vitorja
Senglea
Southeast Malta

The Three Cities on the south side of the Grand Harbour are collectively known as Cottonera because of the line of fortifications that surrounds all three of them, which was built on the orders of Grand Master Nicholas Cotoner. An area with plenty to see, appreciate, and admire. Many visitors are surprised at how much survived the continuous bombing during World War II. The churches, the streets, the views and the fortifications, and Fort St Angelo in particular, are the highlights of this area.

197 ĦAŻ-ŻEBBUĠ

Triq l-Imdina
Ħaż-Żebbuġ
South Malta

One of the oldest and most interesting towns in the country. Originally there were five small hamlets, until they continued to expand, and a large parish church was built in the middle of all five. In addition to the old town centre, which is a hive of activity, there are also the hamlets nearby, as well as the characteristic valleys, that form part of Ħaż-Żebbuġ.

198 ŻEJTUN

Triq Bon Kunsill
Żejtun
Southeast Malta

The oldest archaeological remains in Żejtun go back to the prehistoric period. Roman remains point to the production of olive oil. The small and narrow lanes and streets that wind their way around the village, the various outlying hamlets, forming part of Żejtun, and the small churches are a unique characteristic of this town. Its parish church is considered one of the architectural treasures of Malta. You can continue your walk towards the surrounding coastline from the town. Definitely worth exploring.

CANOEING

ADVENTURES 🦶

W A T E R *adventures*

---

199 **CANOEING**

Ġnejna Bay
Mġarr
Northwest Malta
+356 7959 4000
*gnejnawater
sports.com*

Your best option to appreciate the cliffs and secluded bays of the Maltese Islands is by canoe. Canoeing is becoming ever more popular, and there are several places where you can hire one to go experience Malta's natural beauty. The Ġnejna Bay area and its spectacular limestone cliffs is just one location you should consider exploring.

200 **FLYBOARD MALTA**

Caravel / Triq
Tal-Qattus
Birkirkara
Central Malta
+356 9947 1644
flyboard.com.mt

Looking for a different perspective on the bay where you went for a swim earlier? Try flyboarding for something different and a great adrenaline rush. Fly above the water and learn new skills.

201 **SUP TOURS MALTA**

TOURS AVAILABLE AT
DIFFERENT LOCATIONS
+356 7744 5595
+356 7970 6151
supmalta.com

Stand-Up-Paddling is the latest water craze to have been introduced in Malta. Explore Malta's clear waters and coastline with Pierre Mercieca, who is a licensed tourist guide and lards your tour with interesting anecdotes about the area you are visiting. SUP Tours Malta organises sunrise and sunset tours in various parts of the islands.

202 YACHTING AROUND MALTA

TA' XBIEX MARINA
Ta' Xbiex
Central Malta
+356 9945 1297
ldemajo28@gmail.com

Spend a relaxing day or even several days on a sailing boat, touring the Maltese Islands while being pampered by the yacht owner (Lawrence and his son James), visiting different bays and secluded areas throughout the day and diving in quiet places. Exploring Malta on a yacht is the ultimate relaxing experience and one that you can definitely not afford to miss.

202 YACHTING AROUND MALTA

Adventurous **HIKING** areas

203 **DELIMARA**
Delimara Road
Marsaxlokk
Southeast Malta

Although close to Malta's new power station, there is still a lot of pristine countryside and coastline to explore in Delimara. You can visit part of the British fortifications and even a 19th-century lighthouse. The views from the ridges towards Marsaxlokk Bay and the open seas are simply unique.

204 **L-AHRAX**
Mellieħa
Northwest Malta

A dramatic landscape where you can watch the sea crash into the cliffs on winter days. The area is rich in flora and towards the end of the tip of the peninsula there is a natural hole in the karst from where you can take great photos. Start your walk from Spiaggia del Corallo. This will take you to the tip of the island, where the Coral Lagoon is located.

205 **FAWWARA AREA**
Siġġiewi
South Malta

Right in the middle of the countryside, with few cars to bother you, as you walk past a farmer as he tirelessly works the fields. The Fawwara area is one of those places where you literally feel as if you have travelled back in time two hundred years. You'll run into the usual terraced fields as well as small countryside churches and even cave dwellings.

206 MUNXAR

Triq Ras il-Bajjada
Munxar
Gozo

Start your walk from the parish church of Munxar. Walk down Triq Dun Spir Gauci and follow the signs for Sanap Cliffs. The paved path starts at the edge of the cliffs. A little bit of the path is paved, after which you can easily follow the marked unpaved trail. This hike will take you along the spectacular cliffs towards the splendid Xlendi Bay and its rock formations. End your walk with a refreshing plunge in the clear blue sea and top up your lost moisture . A great hike for those who want to explore Gozo's pristine coastline.

207 TA' ĊENĊ

Triq Ta' Ċenċ
Sannat
Gozo

Escape the hustle and bustle of everyday life and admire this beautiful large expanse of rocky landscape. You'll run into the archaeological remains of Ta' Ċenċ and Borġ l-Imramma along the way, including a megalithic temple and some dolmens, as you walk down to one of Gozo's most idyllic bays, called Mġarr ix-Xini. The sea in this inlet is beautiful, clear and deep.

208 WIED IL-GHASRI

Għasri
Gozo

Start your walk from the centre of the small village of Għasri, winding your way through cultivated fields and a valley and finishing by the sea. At the end of the walk, and at the mouth of the narrow bay, a large arch provides spectacular views, especially when the sea is rough. Continue along the coast, towards Marsalforn. A spectacular walk throughout.

SNORKELLING *and* SCUBA DIVING

Malta's turquoise waters are great for snorkelling but the islands also have more than 25 scuba diving sites, which are suitable for beginners, advanced and technical divers. The dive sites include coral reefs, submerged caves, and scuttled vessels of different sizes and periods. Most of the dive sites can be reached from the shore.

209 ĊIRKEWWA DIVE SITE

Triq il-Marfa
Ċirkewwa
Northwest Malta

This diving area has several assets. Here you can explore natural arches and tunnels, as well as the wrecks of two vessels (the *Rozi*, an old tugboat, and the *P29*, a patrol boat). Both have been colonised by schools of fish, offering an amazing spectacle.

210 PARADISE BAY DIVE SITE

Paradise Bay
Mellieħa
Northwest Malta

Another popular site with divers, both for the experienced and the less experienced. The rock formations here are spectacular, serving as a backdrop to the deep blue sea that surrounds this part of the island with drop-offs of more than 50 metres. The sea is usually very clear, but be warned, the currents can be strong at times.

211 COMINO DIVE SITES
DIFFERENT LOCATIONS
Comino

There are several dive sites in and around Comino, most of which are mainly located away from the popular beach areas, as there are Blue Lagoon, Santa Maria Bay and St Nicholas Bay. Here you can see natural rock formations, caves, reefs that are rich with fish and other interesting sights such as the wreck of the *P31* patrol boat. The island can get quite busy during the summer months. There are more than 12 dive sites around Comino. The majority are submerged caves arches, and reefs. Only one offers the possibility to see the remains of a 19th-century battleship that was shipwrecked on the reef.

212 HMS MAORI
Boat St
Marsamxett
Harbour
Valletta

A popular dive site with a World War II wreck. *HMS Maori* was involved in various sea battles until she was bombed and sunk in 1942 during one of the many air raids against Malta. Her wreck was later raised and now rests on a sandy bed, at a depth of approx. 16 metres. *HMS Maori* provides shelter to hundreds of fish.

BUSKETT GARDENS

LANDSCAPES ▲

CURIOSITIES *worth the detour*

213 BETHLEHEM VILLAGE

Triq L-Imġarr
Ghajnsielem
Gozo
+356 2156 1515
ghajnsielemlc.gov.mt

The small village of Ghajnsielem on Gozo decided that the traditional Christmas manger was not for them. Instead, they reconstructed Bethlehem where Jesus was born two thousand years ago, converting a disused stretch of land into a thriving and busy village. At Christmas and Easter, when the village is open to the public, farm animals roam the village and craftsmen go about their business as actors recreate life as it was all those centuries ago, with a real-life baby being nursed by its mother in a grotto.

214 IL-MAQLUBA

Triq it-Tempesta
Qrendi
South Malta

A natural sinkhole, at the origin of numerous legends. Because of the small medieval chapel that is built on its edge, legend has it that this place was once inhabited by people who lived in sin. God is said to have punished these sinners with an earthquake that engulfed the hamlet. When the villagers arrived in Hell, they were turned away and the village was thrown out into the sea, creating the islet of Filfla off the coast. The sinkhole is a protected area due to the diverse flora and fauna found within it.

215 INLAND SEA

Triq Id-Dwejra
San Lawrenz
Gozo

The coast of the Maltese Islands is very scenic and diverse. One of the most interesting and impressive attractions along the coastline is the Inland Sea in Gozo. An opening formed by a natural arch in the face of a cliff links a lagoon and safe harbour for small boats to the sea. You can sail through the spectacular natural tunnel to the open sea, visiting the interesting sea caves and admiring the natural cliffs. The Inland Sea is also a popular swimming spot – the clear blue water is always relatively calm here.

216 MIĠRA L-FERḤA

Mtaħleb
Rabat
Northwest Malta

Legend has it that this is the spot where Count Roger, the Norman ruler of Sicily, and his army landed in 1091 to free Malta from the Moors. It's glaringly obvious that galleys would never have been able to unload troops and horses here. And yet… The site's name means 'joyous arrival' to denote the jubilant welcome that the count and his men would have received from the locals upon landing. Stunning panoramas and walks guaranteed.

NATURE PARKS
you shouldn't miss

---

217 **BIRD PARK**
Mdawra Road
Burmarrad
Northwest Malta
+356 9986 8608
birdparkmalta.com

A unique place that is home to more than 200 different species of birds and other animals and a great opportunity to learn more about them. Popular with families as it combines recreation with education.

218 **FILFLA**
South Malta

The smallest islet of the Maltese archipelago. Its name suggests that pepper once used to be cultivated here. The islet is a protected site, and therefore access to it is restricted. It is also dangerous due to natural erosion. During the 1950s, British forces used this islet for target practice. There once used to be a small church here, where stranded fishermen could take refuge after being surprised by a storm. Although you cannot actually visit the islet, you can take a boat and sail around it.

219 GHADIRA NATURE RESERVE

Triq Il-Marfa
Mellieħa
Northwest Malta
+356 7955 4347
birdlifemalta.org

One of Malta's most interesting nature reserves. The name 'Għadira' refers to the low-lying wetland with brackish water, which is popular with migrating passerines and an important watering hole and feeding ground for waders. Easy to reach and visit. Depending on the time of year, you can observe all kinds of birds and other wildlife in their natural habitat.

220 MALTA FALCONRY CENTRE

Triq L-Imqabba
Siġġiewi
South Malta
+356 2146 0985
maltafalconry
centre.com

This is the first bird of prey centre to have been established in Malta, inspired by the archipelago's ancient falconry tradition. King Frederick II of Sicily used Malta as a breeding ground for falcons in the 13th century, gifting locally bred falcons to other nobles and monarchs. After Malta was given to the Order of the Knights of St John as a fief by Emperor Charles V, they were expected to pay an annual tribute in the form of one Maltese falcon. See these famous birds of prey up close at the centre where they also offer bird handling sessions.

221 TAS-SIMAR NATURE RESERVE

Triq il-Pwales
St Paul's Bay
Northwest Malta
+356 7953 8122
birdlifemalta.org

This nature reserve is surrounded by well-tended agricultural land. Migrating birds stop here to enjoy the lush surroundings and the wetlands within the reserve. The area is dotted with a number of small open pools, reeds and trees and is teeming with wildlife.

Where to go
WALKING IN NATURE

---

222 BUSKETT GARDENS

Buskett Road
Siġġiewi
South Malta

One of the few woodland areas in Malta and an excellent place to leave the city behind and enjoy a walk in nature. The name is derived from the Italian word *boschetto* which means small wood. There are a number of signposted trails to choose from. The gardens are home to orange trees and other tree species.

223 CHADWICK LAKES

Triq Tas-Slampa
Rabat
Northwest Malta

During the 19th century, dams were built here to retain the limited amount of rainwater that falls in Malta each year, to be used for agricultural purposes. The dams have created several small, artificial lakes in the valleys. A popular spot for hikes and picnics, it also offers a great vantage point to take in the surrounding terraced fields. Along the trails, you'll find signs that provide information about the area's natural environment.

224 GHADIRA TA' SAN RAFFLU

Triq Santa
Katerina Tal
Qabbieza
Kerċem
Gozo

A man-made freshwater pond, that is home to several flora and fauna, some of which are specific to this area. During wintertime the water level is much higher but you'll always find water here, even during the arid summer months. The pond is surrounded by fertile land, making it a good spot for a country walk with spectacular views of the area.

225 FUNGUS ROCK

Triq id-Dwejra
San Lawrenz
Gozo

A walk along the coast is always invigorating. Most visitors stop to admire the Inland Sea, but you can also take a walk along the coast to another bay, called Dwejra. A large rock, known as Fungus Rock, protects the entrance to this bay. Apparently, it is the only place in Malta where a root with medicinal properties grows, which is why this is a protected area. Today Fungus Rock is a nature reserve and off-limits.

223 CHADWICK LAKES

226 TAL-MAJJISTRAL PARK

Il-Kamp ta' Għajn
Tuffieħa
Triq Il – Kappella
Tal-Militar
Manikata
Northwest Malta
+356 2152 1291
majjistral.org

A place where rural nature blends in with cliffs and spectacular views of the nearby bays. This was the first natural national park to be established in Malta. It is also home to a number of archaeological and historical remains. The area is a rich ecologically diverse habitat, making it an interesting place to visit. The archaeological and historical remains range from antiquity to World War II.

227 ANNUNCIATION VALLEY / IL-LUNŻJATA VALLEY

Triq Petri
Victoria
Gozo

This fertile valley, with the continuous sound of water running from the springs and aqueducts that line the valley, supplies water to the very busy farmers that work the fields in it. You enter the park through an arched passageway, where a small chapel dedicated to the Annunciation to Our Lady is situated. An important area for agriculture, the valley also has natural caves that were still used by the local farmers until very recently. A place to enjoy some peace and quiet.

228 XROBB L-GĦAĠIN NATURE PARK

Triq Xrobb
l-Għaġin
Marsaxlokk
Southeast Malta
+356 2165 3851
xrobblghagin.org.mt

This natural park is located in a relatively unspoilt area, with views of the countryside and the white cliffs of Munxar and the Delimara peninsula. The park is also a centre for sustainable development, with on-site educational facilities. You can spend a few days in the park's hostel, in the tranquil countryside by the sea.

Secluded **BAYS**

229 **DAHLET QORROT BAY**

Triq Daħlet Qorrot
Nadur
Gozo

Another secluded inlet on Gozo, with a nice pebbly beach to swim off. To reach the beach you need to walk beyond the caves at the base of the cliffs that have been turned into huts by the local fishermen. Be careful when the sea is rough. The inlet with its clear, deep water is also a popular spot for pleasure boats to drop anchor.

230 **FOMM IR-RIH BAY**

Fomm ir-Riħ Bay
Road
Mġarr
Northwest Malta

A small, secluded bay that is relatively difficult to reach. Walk along the narrow path to reach the bay and enjoy spectacular sea views. Be prepared for the long, arduous walk back up. Time your walk to avoid having to walk in the hot afternoon sun.

231 **ĠEBLA TAL-HALFA**

Limits of Qala
Gozo

Located near Qala, this small, picturesque inlet is protected by a large limestone rock. The rock towers over the small bay, providing shelter from the waves. You can easily swim around it and find a place to climb it for a different view of the islet.

232 GHAR LAPSI

Siġġiewi
South Malta

A rocky beach that is very popular with the locals. Very scenic, with clear and clean blue seas. A great place for snorkelling as well, as the various rock formations provide spectacular views of what lies beneath the sea. The island of Filfla can be seen in the distance.

233 COMINO

Comino

This small island, between the archipelago's two main islands of Malta and Gozo, is well-known for its clear blue seas. The famous Blue Lagoon is always teeming with boats and swimmers. However, there are several other smaller bays around Comino where you can swim in the same clear and clean blue seas, that are less crowded. Also an excellent location for a hike during the cooler months.

232 GHAR LAPSI

234 MISTRA BAY

St Paul's Bay
Northwest Malta

This hidden gem, with a small sandy beach and rocky shoreline, has plenty of places where you can enjoy a dip in the sea. Although it is considered an inlet of the larger St Paul's Bay, this bay is less crowded. Mistra Bay is also a good area for snorkelling.

235 SAN BLAS BAY

Nadur
Gozo

One of Gozo's small, unknown bays and relatively difficult to reach. You have to walk down a very steep narrow path. On reaching the small scenic beach, you'll see why it was worth the effort. Quiet, clean with a mesmerising clear blue sea.

236 ST PETER'S POOL

Marsaxlokk
Southeast Malta

The famous St Peter's Pool, with its deep sea, rocky shoreline and a variety of locations where you test your diving skills in the clear blue sea. Off the beaten track, which is why it is so popular with young people. You can get a boat from Marsaxlokk village to the bay.

Secret GARDENS

237 BIRGU DITCH GARDENS

Couvre Porte
Vittoriosa
Southeast Malta

The moat of the fortified city of Vittoriosa has been restored and filled with trees and paths. An opportunity to admire the city's fortifications, that withstood more than one siege during their centuries-old history. The small doorways are the entrances to the shelters that the locals cut out in the rock during World War II. The garden's entrance is situated next to the main entrance to the city.

237 BIRGU DITCH GARDENS

238 CHINESE GARDEN OF SERENITY

Triq il-Pepprin
Santa Luċija
South Malta
+356 2166 6600

This garden – Malta's only Chinese garden - opened to the public in 1997. Built to the specifications of Chinese garden planning, this garden is designed around three principles. It needs to represent a complete world of balance where thoughts can flow, reflect the local environment (with rocks and water symbolising the opposites of yin and yang), and offer different moods and an opportunity to meditate on life, from birth to death. A place to connect with your spiritual self.

238 CHINESE GARDEN OF SERENITY

239 **CITADEL DITCH**
Victoria
Gozo

The recently restored ditch of the Citadel on Gozo has provided locals and tourists with a quiet garden to relax. You can also admire the medieval and 16th-century fortifications from below. Several tunnels lead into the Citadel. These were meant to be used by the soldiers in case they needed to abandon their front-line positions and return to the safety of the Citadel.

240 **ROMEO ROMANO GARDENS**
Braille St
Santa Venera
Central Malta

These gardens are a godsend, offering respite from the ever-congested city. The gardens are part of a large 18th-century country residence of one of the Grand Masters of the Order of St John. A section of the grounds has been opened to the public. Looking back at the house, you realise that this is terraced garden, always leading down and away from the terrace of the residence.

241 **HASTINGS GARDENS**
Windmill St
Valletta

One of three gardens in Valletta, located on the bastions of the 16th-century city. The gardens were developed in the early years of the British Period. They offer breathtaking views of the suburb of Floriana and Marsamxett Harbour. Less busy than Valletta's other gardens, Hastings Gardens is a quiet place to relax after a day of visiting the city's many attractions.

242 SA MAISON GARDEN

Triq Sa Maison
Floriana
Southeast Malta

Floriana, a suburb of Valletta, has several gardens that are set in the 17th-century fortifications. Sa Maison is the most hidden garden of them all. Set on five levels of fortifications, it boasts superb views of Marsamxett Harbour. Construction began in 1636, but it was only during the 19th century that the fortifications were leased for use as a private garden and residence by Lady Lockwood. The British Army later used this place as a temporary post for troops waiting to be shipped out to other Mediterranean stations. Look out for the many environmental crests that are engraved in the rock in the garden. A good place to retreat in quiet surroundings.

THE POINT SHOPPING MALL

SHOPPING 🛍

The best of Malta's
FASHION SCENE

---

243 CHARLES AND RON
58D Republic St
Valletta
+356 2124 0184
charlesandron.com

A high-end lifestyle brand that remains true to its origins, created by Malta's most sought-after fashion designers. The designers have presented their collections during fashion week in the USA and are regular guests at fashion weeks throughout Europe. Charles and Ron have several shops throughout Malta.

244 PIPPA TOLEDO DESIGN STUDIO
GARDEN TERRACE
COURT
272 Triq il-Baltiku
St Julian's
Central Malta
+356 2132 3616
pippatoledo.com

Unique collections of handmade jewellery, handbags and home decor and accessories, in the designer's inimitable style. The place to shop for a unique gift or that one finishing touch to your interior. Also a great place to find inspiration for your home.

245 THE POINT SHOPPING MALL
Tigné Point
Sliema
+356 2247 0300
thepointmalta.com

Malta's main shopping mall, and home to the largest concentration of exclusive brands, all conveniently located under one roof. A bustling mecca for keen shoppers, offering everything from the latest fashions, jewellery and technology as well as a selection of fast casual and fine dining restaurants, cafes and popup caterers.

OUTDOOR MARKETS

you'll absolutely love

246 BIRGU CAR BOOT SALE

St Edward St
Vittoriosa
Southeast Malta

Traditional car boot/flea markets pop up occasionally throughout the islands, but this is the only one to be held every Sunday, regardless of the weather conditions. The perfect place to score unique or long-forgotten items to add to your collection, drawing both tourists and locals.

246 BIRGU CAR BOOT SALE

247 FARMERS' MARKET

TA' QALI CRAFTS
VILLAGE
Ta' Qali
Attard
Central Malta

Fresh produce, cultivated for you, straight from the farmers. The market is held on Tuesdays and Saturdays near an abandoned airfield, and it stretches for quite a distance.

248 STREET MARKET

Popular street markets are held throughout the archipelago, in the larger towns, on various weekdays. Besides the one in Valletta, there are also markets in Żejtun, Qormi, Rabat and Gozo. You'll find a variety of stalls at these outdoor markets, selling all kinds of merchandise, from clothes, food, household things and others.

249 FISH MARKET

Xatt is-Sajjieda
Marsaxlokk
Southeast Malta

On Sundays, Marsaxlokk, Malta's largest fishing village, hosts the only outdoor fish market on the island. Here you can buy fresh fish, and sometimes spot fishermen unloading their catch. The fresh fish on offer varies according to season. Settle on a price and the stallholder will clean your fish so you can take it home and cook it to your liking. Alternatively, head to one of the many fish restaurants in the town if you don't feel like cooking. Don't forget to take a walk past the typical colourful fishing boats.

Original SOUVENIRS to bring back

250 BRISTOW POTTERIES
TA' QALI CRAFTS VILLAGE
Attard
Central Malta
+356 2142 1473
bristowpotteries.com

One of the oldest manufacturers of ceramics in Malta, this family-run business was founded in 1972. At any given time, they have more than 700 artistic products on display at their shop and factory, where you can admire the many different colours that are produced on site. They also do custom designs.

251 MDINA GLASS
TA' QALI CRAFTS VILLAGE
Attard
Central Malta
+356 2141 5786
mdinaglass.com.mt

Malta's oldest glassworks produces exquisitely decorated, handblown glassware, with rich colours and unique shapes and designs. Visit the shop and factory where you can see the artisans at work. The items on display include smaller items as well magnificent large pieces of glassware. A must-visit.

252 MALTA FILIGREE

You can find handcrafted Malta filigree in all the main shopping centres such as Valletta and Sliema. A tradition that may been inherited from the ancient Phoenicians, filigree jewellery is exquisite, intricate and widely reputed. Shop for small souvenirs to bring home to family or friends or other unique pieces.

253 HERITAGE HOMES

TA' QALI CRAFTS
VILLAGE
Attard
Central Malta
+356 9949 6994

Popular miniature and historical buildings are brought to life in these exquisitely created, colourful creations. The miniatures range from the great monumental buildings and fortifications that dot the islands to the small unpretentious rural buildings, farmhouses and other streetscapes that are so typical of Maltese villages.

254 MEDITERRANEAN CERAMICS

Pinto Wharf /
Valletta
Waterfront
Floriana
Southeast Malta
+356 2122 6782
mediterranean
ceramics.com

The techniques and colour schemes used for these handmade ceramics are of Mediterranean inspiration. This family-run business is inspired by international artists, creating their own unique styles while drawing on local traditions. A great place to shop for decorative ceramics, household ceramics and other pieces of colourful ceramics for outdoor use.

255 VILLA BOLOGNA POTTERY

St Anthony St
Attard
Central Malta
+356 9953 7925
villabologna.com

This pottery producer moved into the old stables of an 18th-century stately home, with stunning gardens, which is also open to the public. Originally established in the 1920s, the pottery's output has continued to evolve over the years, with different shapes and designs. Every piece is handcrafted by slip casting white earthenware clay. Pop into the small souvenir shop with its dazzling array of colourful pieces before you leave.

256 GEORGE ZAMMIT HERB SHOP

St Paul's St
Valletta
+356 2123 6553

As you walk down to the harbour, your nose may detects different smells wafting towards you. You are walking past the spice shop, the only one of its kind in Malta, which has been in business for more than 130 years and is still family-owned. No pre-packed sachets of herbs here. Simply buy the quantity you need, which is presented to you in the old-fashioned way – wrapped in greaseproof paper. Stop in to enjoy the myriad of smells.

TRABUXU BISTRO

FOOD 🍴

AUTHENTIC MALTESE
eateries

---

257 DIAR IL-BNIET

Triq il-Kbira
Dingli
Northwest Malta
+356 2762 0727
diarilbniet.com

The name of this restaurant derives from the title of a medieval fief, located in the area. The fertile land is still used for growing produce, and this is one of the best assets of this restaurant, as they serve fresh vegetables and other local products, 'from their fields to your fork'. The decoration of the restaurant is that of a typical old Maltese eatery, combined with the delicious smells wafting into the dining room from the kitchen and the sweets on offer. They also organise culinary workshops. Booking is recommended.

258 IL-BARRI

Triq il-Kbira
Mġarr
Northwest Malta
+356 2157 3235
il-barri.com.mt

Just off the main square of this village, this is also one of the first restaurants to open in this locality. They have been in business for 75 years, and it is still a family-run restaurant. As it caters to a more Maltese clientele, the portions are large, and good. One of its mainstays is the rabbit stew. Another attraction is the underground World War II shelter, which lies beneath the restaurant.

259 TA' RIKARDU

4 Fosos St
Victoria
Gozo
+356 2155 5953

The place to have lunch or dinner, in the Citadel. A restaurant that has retained part of the original decor, serving tasty local favourites, whether vegetable soup or rabbit stew. A popular place, also for its appetisers, and in particular the local cheese and wine from the owner's vineyard and farm.

260 IL-BITHA TA' DONI

St Paul's St
Rabat
Northwest Malta
+356 2761 5270

Located on one of the busy streets of Rabat, between traditional buildings and a small church, the restaurant offers a good ambience, and a relaxed atmosphere as well as good authentic Maltese and Mediterranean food.

261 TA' MARIJA RESTAURANT

Constitution St
Mosta
Northwest Malta
+356 2143 4444
tamarija.com

Ta' Marija offers a unique experience, with abundant authentic Maltese fare, gastro-style cuisine and a folklore show and music for your enjoyment. The restaurant's success is due in part to the fact that it's still family-owned, making it a popular choice with both locals and visitors.

Your daily **BREAD**

There are still a good number of bakeries around the small villages of Malta and Gozo, that sell authentic baked treats and savouries, with the traditional atmosphere that was so commonplace till a few years ago. Some of these bakeries have updated their product range to satisfy modern requirements.

262 **MAXOKK BAKERY**
St James St
Nadur
Gozo
+356 2155 0014
maxokkbakery.com

This is a family-run bakery, well-known for their local and traditional *ftira*, the Maltese equivalent of a pizza. However, the ingredients, texture and taste are different from the traditional pizza. The only way to find out is to taste one. Try one with the local cheeselets. *Ftira* is oven-baked in the old brick oven, which helps to retain the traditional taste.

263 **MEKREN BAKERY**
Triq Ħanaq
Nadur
Gozo
+356 2155 2342

A favourite place to stop in and pick up freshly baked bread, or ricotta pies and even pizzas, baked in the old oven that is still in use, before continuing your visit of Gozo. A family-run bakery, located in an old building, which has been in use by the family for a number of years.

264 NENU THE ARTISAN BAKER

143 St Dominic St
Valletta
+356 2258 1535
nenuthebaker.com

Located in an old bakery, which supplied the daily bread to the local community of downtown Valletta, this has since been turned into a classic Maltese restaurant. You can still visit the bakery, and it has been done up to show visitors how bread was prepared here. The food on offer is traditional and the local Maltese names have been retained to add more flavour. The atmosphere and the food take you back in time, albeit in a modernised setting. Booking is recommended.

265 TA' SAMINU BAKERY

Soil St
Xewkija
Gozo
+356 2156 0864
tasaminubakery.com

A small traditional bakery selling freshly baked bread, savouries, and pastries. The place is usually busy, and you can usually catch customers looking at the freshly baked products, smelling the still hot bread, and buying and sampling different freshly baked products. No seating.

TRADITIONAL MALTESE FARE *you should try*

Malta has a nice variety of traditional snacks and food, that is appreciated by the locals and visitors alike. Although many of these snacks can be bought from local snack bars, you can also find them as streetfood.

266 HOBŻ BIŻ-ŻEJT

Enter any bar or snack bar, and they are bound to offer you some delicious *hobż biż-żejt* – meaning a small loaf of bread with olive oil. The open sandwich is prepared by pouring olive oil onto the bread, followed by a sweetish tomato paste, and topped with tuna, capers, olives and other ingredients depending on your taste. Locals take this to the beach as a snack. Try it, and wash it down with a beer.

267 ORANGES

Good local oranges, some of which are blood red. These are very tasty but they taste even better when peeled and eaten rather than squeezed for their juice. It is believed that this fruit was introduced about a thousand years ago by the Arabs. Still very popular today.

268 **PRICKLY PEARS**

This seasonal fruit is quite delicious. These are served already peeled, and are usually kept in the fridge. They will taste even better. Cactus plants can be found all over the countryside, and in season you may even spot their colourful fruit. These plants are also used as a barrier between fields, to ward off intruders. In recent years a liquor made from this fruit has been introduced to market.

269 **RABBIT STEW**

So many restaurants offer this popular Maltese dish. The staple for a dinner with a group of friends, to celebrate something. Rabbit stew can also be served fried. Usually, it comes with various vegetables, but they are of secondary importance. Feel free to eat the rabbit with your hands, as that is the best way to enjoy rabbit stew. Wash down your stew with some delicious Maltese wine.

268 PRICKLY PEARS

270 **QUBBAJT**

This is the local nougat, sweet, and made with different ingredients, in different shapes and colours. You will find stalls selling this nougat at the local religious feasts. The vendors usually let you taste before buying. The Maltese say that a feast without tasting this sweet is no feast at all.

271 **STREET FOOD**

What can you expect to buy on the street? Essentially, anything imaginable. Some street vendors sell the usual burgers, pies and ice cream. Then there are those who are more traditional, selling the traditional *pastizzi*, the cheese or pea puff pastry, the *imqaret*, a pastry stuffed with fried dates, and even homemade drinks. They are everywhere you look and you'll usually find a fair share of them at religious feasts.

Dining with a **SEA VIEW**

272 **SOTTOVENTO**
Xatt il-Forn
Vittoriosa
Southeast Malta
+356 2180 8990

One of the best fish restaurants in the area. It provides excellent and comfortable seating, besides having spacious premises, both outside and indoors. The fish dishes are very good, and the fish on offer is super fresh. The menu includes other traditional fare, that is both popular with the locals and visitors. A place to visit.

272 SOTTOVENTO

273 BIRGU WHARF

Xatt il-Forn
Vittoriosa
Southeast Malta

Along the modernised wharf of Vittoriosa, the former headquarters of the fleets of the Knights of Malta and the British Navy, you can find several good places to stop and have lunch and bask in the afternoon sun or have dinner. You overlook the inner part of Dockyard Creek, with its many sailing boats, and the surrounding maritime area. The restaurants in the area serve all kinds of food, whether the local snack, or even pizzas, fish and meat dishes. There is a wide variety of restaurants to choose from.

274 COAST @ CASSARINI

Triq Is-Sajjieda
Wied iż-Żurrieq
Qrendi
South Malta
+356 9920 7911
coast-com.mt

This is one of those places where the land encounters the beautiful shoreline and the sea. On sunny days, head for a table up on the terrace, to enjoy the scenery and sunset. The food here is traditional but inspired by international cuisine as well. The restaurant is located in a small hamlet, built around the inner part of creek, perfect for a short walk before or after your meal. Visiting in the morning? Consider taking a boat ride to the famous Blue Grotto.

275 TARTARUN

20 Xatt is-Sajjieda
Marsaxlokk
Southeast Malta
+356 2165 8089
tartarun.com

Situated in Malta's largest fishing village, the restaurant boasts that it is also one of the best fish restaurants on the island. The varied menu includes a selection of traditional and culinary delights, as well as a nice wine list. Booking is recommended.

276 HAMMETT'S MACINA

Triq il-31 Ta' Marzu
Xatt Juan B
Azopardo
Senglea
Southeast Malta
+356 2779 4171
hammetts
macina.com

A restaurant that combines a historic building with the unique scenery of a busy creek within the Three Cities. The menu is a mix of local culinary traditions, larded with influences from the various European and Mediterranean powers that occupied the islands throughout the centuries. A taste of history!

277 SENGLEA WHARF

Xatt Juan B
Azopardo
Senglea
Southeast Malta

Facing the city of Vittoriosa, Senglea has a wharf lined with eateries. Plenty of places to choose from and most of them have indoor or outdoor seating. During the warm summer months, the area can get busy – with people enjoying a stroll along the wharf, eating, or even playing bingo. A bustling seafront and there is always some entertainment going on during the summer months.

278 VALLETTA WATERFRONT

Triq il-Vittmi tal-
Gwerra Furjanizi
Floriana
Southeast Malta

Eighteenth-century warehouses, which were modernised to provide services to the cruise liner terminal, and warehouses that have been converted into to restaurants. The location is excellent as it faces the Grand Harbour. There is a wide variety of good food to choose from, and the area is one of the most popular for lunch or an evening dinner. Very popular with the locals.

LUNCH & BRUNCH

279 CULTO CAFFETTERIA-PANINERIA

49 St John's St
Valletta
+356 2749 6810

While walking and exploring the magnificent baroque city of Valletta, stop and have a bite or a sandwich in a typical Italian-style cafe. This small eatery is an excellent place to stop in between visits to the various sites in Valletta.

280 GIORGIO'S CAFETERIA

17 Tigne St
Sliema
Central Malta
+356 2134 2456

A good place to relax, in the centre of Sliema's busy shopping centre. Giorgio's serves good lunches, snacks and sweets as well. The portions are large, so pay attention when you order, so as not to waste food. The place is popular with locals meaning you may find it difficult to bag a seat. Open till late, good for a late dinner.

279 CULTO CAFFETTERIA-PANINERIA

Places for **FOODIES**

281 CAROB TREE

Triq Mikiel'Ang Borg
St Julian's
Central Malta
+356 9947 0460
carobtree.com.mt

A food court in the centre of St Julian's, with plenty of options to choose from. The 11 kitchens and bars offer a wide range of food and drinks. Located within easy reach from the coastline of St Julian's, this is a good place to stop in the afternoon, or in the evening for a relaxing meal at the end of a hectic day.

282 IS-SUQ TAL-BELT

Merchants St
Valletta
+356 2210 3500

This food court is located within the old 19th-century market of Valletta, which has recently been restored. There are a number of restaurants that offer a wide range of food – whether snacks, or a proper meal with meat and fresh fish. There is seating all around, and you can sit anywhere, including outside. There is also a supermarket on the lower level.

Special food and drinks for
MALTESE FESTIVITIES

283 GĦADAM TAL-MEJTIN

This is a typical sweet, usually only eaten in the month of November, the month during which Christians remember their dearly departed. The sweet is formed to resemble a human bone – and called *għadam tal-mejtin*, literally meaning bones of the dead. The flavourful shortcrust biscuit is usually filled with crushed almonds, then covered with icing. Very tasty.

284 IMBULJUTA

This is a typical Christmas soup, usually offered after midnight mass at Christmas and at New Year's Eve. Sometimes it is also presented as a hot drink, but with the same ingredients. It is made from chestnuts, which are usually first soaked in order to make them tender. The chestnuts are boiled, along with caster sugar and cocoa powder and tangerine peel, ready to be served as a welcoming warm drink. Nowadays you can buy this soup ready-made, so you only need to warm it up.

285 PRINJOLATA

Malta's favourite Carnival cake. As is the case for so many sweets, everyone uses different recipes and ingredients. However, the basic ingredients are always the same. This looks like a decorative pudding, more colourful than the Christmas pudding. Crushed biscuits, sugar, eggs and vanilla extract are mixed and shaped in a dome, which is then covered with cream frosting and decorated with cherries and pine nuts.

285 PRINJOLATA

UNUSUAL PLACES *to eat*

286 CHOCOLATE DISTRICT

Melita St
Valletta
+356 2788 8668
choclatedistrict.com

Who doesn't like chocolate? This is one of the latest outlets to specialise in chocolate and its various by-products. Besides the international varieties of chocolate on offer, you can taste the local variant as well. While sampling and appreciating the goods, enjoy a coffee or another drink in the small and intimate cafeteria.

286 CHOCOLATE DISTRICT

287 AMBROSIA

137 Archbishop St
Valletta
+356 2122 5923
ambrosia.com.mt

Situated right in the centre of Valletta, next to the Grand Master's Palace, Ambrosia offers a dining experience with a twist. The ambience is different and particular for Valletta. The food is delicious and the portions sizeable. After lunch, you can continue to explore Valletta, or if you had dinner, enjoy a relaxing walk through Valletta's streets.

288 CAFE JUBILEE

Independence
Square
Victoria
Gozo
+356 2133 7141

The original concept was introduced in Gozo, and since then, a number of other outlets have opened, with a couple abroad as well. The interior decoration is different than usual, with an old, nostalgic feel, with posters of theatre productions, adverts as well as items hanging from the ceiling or on shelves. The food is good, different and very tasty as well. This outlet has tables inside as well as outside seating in the main square of Victoria.

289 DEL BORGO

33 St Dominic St
Vittoriosa
Southeast Malta
+356 9944 7954
delborgomalta.com

The quiet narrow streets of Vittoriosa have a number of different locations where you can stop for a good meal. This particular wine bar and eatery in an old building is unique. It provides a different kind of seating – for those who are sitting down to a meal and for those who are there to socialise around a bottle or two of good wine, with some cheese and other nibbles. Very popular with the locals.

290 FONTANELLA TEA GARDEN

1 Bastion St
Mdina
Northwest Malta
+356 2145 4264
fontanellatea
garden.com

Stop for a coffee, a beer or a refreshing drink on the bastions of the old medieval city of Mdina and enjoy the magnificent views. Try the cakes, which are very popular. Next door there is a wine bar, which is a good place in the evening when the city of Mdina is less busy and more relaxing. A favourite.

291 VICTORY CAFÉ

MALTA AT WAR MUSEUM
Couvre Porte
Vittoriosa
Southeast Malta
+356 2180 0992
maltaatwar
museum.com

Pay a visit to one of Malta's best war museums, with a walk through the rock-cut shelters where the locals lived during the three years of constant air-raid attacks. Then stop for a coffee or a beer in the delightfully decorated interior of their coffee shop. A place to pick up some good memorabilia with a small book shop.

292 TA' RINALDU

220 Merchants St
Valletta
+356 7745 6677
tarinaldu.com

Tired from visiting Valletta's many museums, churches and various historical locations? Take a break and stop for lunch or some nibbles at Ta' Rinaldu. Besides the limited outdoor seating that they provide, the interior of this building is interesting, as it gives you an opportunity to discover the local architectural styles that are so typical of 17th-and 18th-century houses. They also serve a wide range of snacks.

293 STAZZJON RESTAURANT

Triq Għajn
Hammam
Rabat
Northwest Malta
+356 2145 1984

This restaurant is located in an old railway station, and the interior is decorated with photos of the old railway, which closed in 1931. The building combines parts of the old railway station with more modern sections. Good parking, away from the busy Mdina and Rabat area. Stazzjon serves a varied lunch and dinner menu.

294 IL VEDUTA PIZZERIA AND RESTAURANT

Is-Saqqajja
Rabat
Northwest Malta
+356 2145 4666
veduta.com.mt

What a magnificent view this place has, overlooking a good part of Malta. While the view at lunch is great, it's even better at night with the twinkling lights of the surrounding villages. In summer, you may even catch one of the fireworks displays that are organised during the village feasts. A good menu, that caters to everyone's taste.

294 IL VEDUTA PIZZERIA AND RESTAURANT

Places with good
VEGETARIAN *options*

---

295 **DANNY'S MALTA**
Imriehel Bypass
Qormi
South Malta
+356 2144 1171
dannys.com.mt

Something different for lunch or a snack. Danny's also serves gluten-free and vegetarian food, preparing and presenting the food in a modern way. You can either book a table or order online for takeaway.

296 **SAPANA INDIAN**
Triq il-Għajn
Xlendi
Gozo
+356 2156 2100
sapana
restaurant.com

The name of the restaurant means 'dream' in Hindu, and it promises to be a culinary dream for those who stop by. The restaurant is located just a few metres from the bay of Xlendi, a popular bay to swim and relax while in Gozo. The only Indian restaurant in Gozo.

297 **SOUL FOOD**
76 Merchants St
Valletta
+356 2123 4311

The mindset behind the concept of this restaurant is to offer tasty and healthy food, including vegetarian, Indian-inspired and other healthy food. It is located on one of the main streets of Valletta, just behind the Grand Master's Palace, and close to the city's other cultural and historical venues.

Where the **L O C A L S** *eat*

---

298 FINS & GILS – FISH AND CHIPS
Mosta Road
St Paul's Bay
Northwest Malta
+356 2713 9297

A typical and popular fish and chips shop, where everything is prepared on site. Its popularity is due to the no-frills offering, and the use of fresh local fish, in addition to the different specials on offer, as well as the large portions. Always popular with the locals.

299 GLENEAGLES BAR
10 Triq il-Vittorja
Għajnsielem
Gozo
+356 2155 6543

This is one of those places where you literally have no idea what hit you the minute you cross the threshold – with the simple fishermen-style decor, the clientele and the atmosphere. A taste of Gozo where the robust atmosphere is part of the experience. The place to stop for a good drink before boarding the ferry back to Malta.

300 IL GOLOSO GELATERIA
Wied iż-Żurrieq
Qrendi
South Malta

This is a small family run ice-cream shop. It offers a wide range of flavours, good portions and very genuine product as well. A popular place to stop for an ice cream during the hot summer months, but just as pleasant in the evening, when the shop is less hectic and more relaxing. The place to go to have ice cream on the rocks and by the sea.

301 TEPIE'S BAR

St Francis Square
Victoria
Gozo

This is an old-style bar, with patrons enjoying a coffee, tea or better still a beer, on chairs just outside the bar, watching the world pass and living the good life. It doesn't get more local than this bar.

302 TRABUXU BISTRO

2 Strait St
Valletta
+356 2122 3036
trabuxu.com.mt

If you like cheese and wine, look no further. A popular place with the locals, that serves cheese as well as cured meats and salami. For those who appreciate good food and excellent wine.

302 **TRABUXU BISTRO**

Where to SAMPLE LOCAL PRODUCE

303 THE MAGRO FOOD VILLAGE

XEWKIJA INDUSTRIAL ESTATE
Xewkija
Gozo
+356 2155 6663
magro.com.mt

When in Gozo, drop by the Magro Food Village where you can visit the factory and see how products are produced and taste some of the products made here. Local and fresh ingredients only, which explains their popularity and success.

304 MALTA SUNRIPE

237 Triq San Pietru
Mġarr
Northwest Malta
+356 2158 3269
maltasunripe.com

This family-run agricultural company offers locally grown produce to their customers. All the products are free from additives and preservatives and hand-picked. Maltese farming at its best.

305 MANINI PUB AND RESTAURANT

Triq L-Avukat
Anton Galea
Kerċem
Gozo
+356 9942 0343

Drop by for a cold beer during summertime, and then book a table for an evening meal. Nothing fancy. The authentic food is cooked the traditional Maltese way, and their rabbit stew is excellent. Meals are served with an abundance of local fresh bread, to be washed down with the local beer or wine. Do try!

306 PERISTYLE RESTAURANT

Museum Esplanade
Rabat
Northwest Malta
+356 2145 6377

Stop by for a coffee, or even for lunch in this spacious restaurant, which is very popular with Maltese patrons. The food is very good, while the local *pastizzi* are excellent as well. Although it can get busy here at lunch, it is still a good place to taste traditional fare.

307 TAL-PETUT

20 P Scicluna St
Vittoriosa
Southeast Malta
+356 7942 1169
talpetut.com

The menu is always limited because they choose to work with local and seasonal products only. The food is cooked the traditional way. They also cater for private functions, or even for small groups. The interior is well decorated, making Tal-Petut feel like a welcoming and warm home. Booking is recommended.

308 AGAPE

25 Triq San Kataldu
Rabat
Northwest Malta
+356 7945 5438
lagapemalta.com

This place prides itself that it offers traditional and local produce. The small menu varies, according to the seasonality of the produce. The owners adhere to the Zero-kilometre principle, sourcing their ingredients from local farmers. Also a place for local artists to showcase their work.

309 VERDALAT – ST JOSEPH FARMHOUSE

Buskett Road
Rabat
Northwest Malta
+356 2145 3613

Going towards Buskett, just before the main entrance of Verdala Palace, one of the official residences of the President of the Republic of Malta, you will find a farmhouse that specialises in the production of fresh Maltese cheeselets, called *ġbejniet*. You can see how these cheeselets are produced, and even buy some freshly made ones to take home. Eat with some fresh Maltese bread.

310 TA' VICTOR RESTAURANT

36 Pjazza Madonna
Ta' Pompei
Marsaxlokk
Southeast Malta
+356 9947 4249

Enjoy a good lunch in the bustling village square, while people flock to the market at the other end of the square. This restaurant specialises in traditional Maltese cuisine, and fish in particular, which they source from local fishermen. A quaint place for a relaxing lunch. On Sundays, take a stroll along the nearby fish market.

GUGAR HANGOUT AND BAR

DRINK 🍷

Sandy feet and delicious drinks
ON THE BEACH

311 **BAIA BEACH CLUB**
Little Armier Bay
Mellieħa
Northwest Malta
+356 2157 0942

An amazing location, overlooking the open sea and the channel between Malta and Gozo, with unique views of Comino, which sits in between the two. This beach club has got everything you need to enjoy a perfect day at the beach including good food and drinks. Famous for its cocktails.

312 **CAFÉ DEL MAR**
MALTA NATIONAL
AQUARIUM
Triq it-Trunċiera
Qawra
Northwest Malta
+356 2258 8100
cafedelmar.com.mt

Part of the National Aquarium, which is popular with families, with the bonus of having an excellent place to relax and enjoy a refreshing drink. Offering unobstructed views of the sea, Café del Mar is an ideal place to relax in the evening and wind down after a day of exploring. The bar is closed during winter season, open from April to October.

313 **CRAB SHELL KIOSK**
Xwenji Bay
Marsalforn
Żebbuġ
Gozo
+356 7904 7262

Away from busy nearby Marsalforn, this tiny but interesting kiosk is a fun place to stop for a drink and enjoy the sea and the nearby salt pans after having walked along the shore, or having a good swim in the quiet bay.

314 MUNCHIES

Marfa Road
Mellieħa
Northwest Malta
+356 2157 6416
munchies.com.mt

A place for all seasons, where you can enjoy a drink or some nibbles while looking at the sea in beautiful Mellieħa Bay. Spend a relaxed day on the beach during the summer months or have a cosy meal with a view inside during the colder months. Book before going.

315 TORTUGA BEACH

Little Armier Bay
Mellieħa
Northwest Malta
+356 2152 2220
tortuga.mt

A day at the beach, relaxing in the sun, the sea and the lido, close to a great place for a refreshing drink. Ample parking space and countryside and sea views. Located in a secluded part of a bay, Tortuga is an excellent place to unwind and enjoy everything that the sea has to offer.

314 MUNCHIES

316 RIVIERA MARTINIQUE

Għajn Tuffieħa Bay
Mellieħa
Northwest Malta
+356 2157 8586

Walk down the many steps to the beach, to enjoy the sea and sand and relax at this small place, which serves good food and drinks with excellent service. A great sunset stop.

317 THE CLIFFS

Triq Panoramika
Dingli
Northwest Malta
+356 2145 5470
thecliffs.com.mt

This place is easy to get to (including by public transport) and there is ample parking. Take a walk along the cliffs, amongst the highest points of the islands and stop for a good meal or a drink. The food and service come highly recommended and the sunsets are breathtaking. Book well in advance, so as not to be disappointed.

A roundup of **LOCAL WINES** and **WINERIES**

---

318 **MERIDIANA WINE ESTATE**

Ta' Qali
Attard
Central Malta
+356 2141 3550
meridiana.com.mt

One of the latest additions to Malta's wine scene, producing premium-quality, unique wines. The winery is set amongst vineyards, and the terrace where tasting sessions are organised boasts a great view of the surrounding countryside and the imposing medieval city of Mdina. The setting is unique and pleasant, and the wines superb.

319 **TA' BETTA WINE ESTATES**

Taż-Żiri, off Triq
Blat il-Qamar
Girgenti, Siġġiewi
South Malta
+356 7977 4477
tabetta.com

They have been producing wine in this location, on a terraced hill, with the nearby Laferla Cross for several years already. The tasting room at this family-owned boutique winery is small and exclusive, giving visitors an opportunity to enjoy the wines in tranquillity, while taking in the countryside and vineyard where they were produced with the medieval town of Mdina as a backdrop.

320 TAL-MASSAR WINERY

Trejqa tas-Sisien
Għarb
Gozo
+356 9986 3529
tal-massarwinery.
business.site

A small, family-owned vineyard, offering vineyard tours. The service at this boutique winery is very personal and excellent. Sample their wines and try some local food products, while listening to a description of the wines that you enjoy.

320 TAL-MASSAR WINERY

COFFEE *and* CAFES

321 BELLUSA CAFE
**Independence
Square
Victoria
Gozo
+356 2155 6243**

Strategically located on a corner, overlooking the ever-busy Independence Square, one of the busiest parts of Victoria, and the narrow streets of the old town. A place that is frequented by tourists, Maltese on holiday or even locals – which explains the mix of languages and dialects you will hear as you sip your java.

322 BUNNA CAFÈ
**38A Republic St
Victoria
Gozo
+356 2705 4215**

Italian-owned and the place to go for a relaxing coffee and snack, while visiting the Citadel or Victoria or to give your feet a rest after your visit. They serve good coffee and some small snacks. Popular with the locals.

323 CAPITAN SPRISS
**66 Main Gate St
Victoria
Gozo
+356 2156 9112**

At first glance, this place looks like a cubby hole beneath another building, but the ambience, the food and the service are all very good. The menu includes a wide range of typical Maltese drinks and delicacies, as well as popular Italian snacks, as this place is also owned by Italians.

324 DEBBIE'S CAFÉ

Gorg Borg Olivier St
Mellieħa
Northwest Malta
+356 2765 4101

The place to stop for a good cup of coffee or tea, as well as kinds of snacks and sweets. A cosy, homely place, that serves a vast selection of breakfasts. Well known for its large portions and value for money.

325 DOLCI PECCATI

268 Tower Road
Sliema
Central Malta
+356 2702 3202
dolcipeccati
malta.com

Sweet sins – a little cafe with loads of snacks and desserts that look so tempting that you will want to try them all. A very popular place, they have two other outlets in other parts of the island, to cater to their dedicated clientele.

326 FRENCH AFFAIRE

Tigné Point
Sliema
+356 7999 0992
frenchaffaire.com.mt

Need a break after shopping? French Affaire has your back, serving coffee or tea if you prefer. The first and original location, although others have since opened because the concept proved so successful. Besides drinks, they also serve a wide range of sweets and snacks.

327 JACOB'S BREW

144 Triq is-Salini
Marsaskala
Southeast Malta
+356 2163 7259

A small, family-run coffee shop, with a twist. Malta's first social enterprise, where they believe in paying it forward, collecting funds to help families facing trauma and delivering free sandwiches and coffee to people in the Intensive Therapy Unit waiting area at the nearby hospital. Enjoy good coffee and snacks as well as service with a smile.

328 JALIE'S COFFEE, CAKES AND BAKES

Triq Tommasso
Dingli
Northwest Malta
+356 2143 4590

Stop in the idyllic village at this amazing little cafe, that faces the square, which is dominated by the 17th-century Parish Church of St Mary. The place to go for a good breakfast, or even an afternoon tea, with scones, sandwiches and sweets.

325 DOLCI PECCATI

English-style **P U B S**

---

329 THE PUB
136 Archbishop St
Valletta
+356 7905 2522

One of the first English-style traditional watering holes to open in Valletta. Unfortunately also the renowned last stop for the legendary actor Oliver Reed, who died here while having a drink one evening during the filming of *Gladiator*. The usual variety of good beers and drinks and pub food. A great little hangout for a beer, offering a great night out.

330 THE QUEEN
VICTORIA CITY
PUB
20 South St
Valletta
+356 9969 8150

The latest English-style pub to open in Valletta, already very popular with clients of all ages. With all the cosiness of an English local, this pub is a great place to go for a good beer and all the usual food classics as well as traditional Maltese grub. Conveniently located on a car-free street, this place is usually busy during the evenings.

FRESHLY SQUEEZED

juices

---

331 DR JUICE

54 Gżira Road
Gżira
Central Malta
+356 2134 1218

A fun place if you're up for something different, whether a light, savoury snack or a drink made with the freshest of fruit. The menu here clearly caters to a health-conscious clientele. Very popular with the locals too, with several outlets around Malta.

332 ĠUGAR HANGOUT AND BAR

89-A Republic St
Valletta
+356 2703 2837

The word 'Ġugar' comes from the Hindi concept of *jugaar*. Although there is no exact English equivalent of the word, *jugaar* is the art of making things work, which is exactly what they do here. A small place, away from the crowds, with a relaxed, friendly atmosphere in downtown Valletta. A great place to hang out, with a cup of coffee or tea and enjoy some good food. A highly recommended place for an afternoon stop after visiting the historical places in Valletta.

333 MINT

Luzio Junction /
Stella Maris St
Sliema
Central Malta
+356 2133 7177
mintmalta.com

This waterfront cafe specialises in the freshest, seasonal and local cuisine. All their delicious smoothies are made to order, and you can add any ingredient you want. Sit down and enjoy a rest after a hectic day, or grab a smoothie to take away. They also serve a nice selection of great-tasting cakes and sweets.

334 PURE JUICE BAR

High St
Sliema
Central Malta
+356 2713 6306
pure.com.mt

A bar for healthy, homemade juices, serving a wide range of snacks, drinks and sweets. Off the beaten track, but still close enough to the main shopping centre of Sliema. A good place to taste the mouth-watering juices and food, made with the freshest ingredients only. Did we mention the sweets?

332 ĠUGAR HANGOUT AND BAR

Malta's CRAFT BEER scene

335 THE BREWHOUSE
CENTRAL BUSINESS
DISTRICT
Mdina Road, Zone 2
Birkirkara
Central Malta
+356 9988 9307
thebrewhouse
malta.com

The first brewery to be established on the island in 1928, which is renowned for its award-winning local beers. A great favourite with the locals as well as with visitors. The group also represents several international brands. Their products can be found all over the islands, at any small, local and chic place. Check out the brewery experience during your visit to learn more about the history of this important local institution.

336 LORD CHAMBRAY BREWERY
Mġarr Road
Xewkija
Gozo
+356 2155 4324
lord-chambray.com

A young dynamic brewery and Malta's first craft beer brewery. The brewery welcomes visitors for tours, during which you can sample their varied products. A small brewery, but with the potential to expand.

337 THE BREW
74 The Strand
Sliema
Central Malta
+356 2703 0398
thebrewmalta.com

A craft beer that is lovingly brewed and served specifically in one location, close to the seafront, near vibrant Sliema. The family-run micro-brewery believes in a personal touch. The Brew is famous for brewing its own beer in the restaurant, which serves food that pairs beautifully with the brews. Booking recommended.

338 THE PHOENIX RAW BEER

Triq il-Burmarrad
Naxxar
Northwest Malta
+356 9971 9278

This is a family-run microbrewery, run by a husband-and-wife team. Alessandro and Federica produce several beers and their products have become well-known and appreciated by local beer fans. They boast that their beverages are brewed with their heart and soul, making them different from the industrial-produced beers. They only make use of the best products, continually experimenting to achieve even better results.

339 STRETTA CRAFT BEER

95 Parallel
Triq il-Baħar l-Iswed
St Julian's
Central Malta
+356 7926 4433
strettacraftbeer.com

This is the personal endeavour of one man who wanted to experiment and launch a good beer. The name, Stretta, is the Maltese word for Strait Street in Valletta, where his family used to live. This craft beer is popular with aficionados of craft beers and always gets good reviews, especially at festivals. A beer to be savoured.

340 THE HUSKIE CRAFT BEER

GARAGE 5, LEVEL-1
Sqaq il-Mithna
Qrendi
South Malta
+356 9927 2888
huskiecraft.com

A small brewery that was originally established in the UK before the two founders and friends decided to move to Malta realising that there was a market for excellent craft beer waiting to be conquered. They have used their international expertise to create better brews, continuing to experiment and create more brews.

Drinks WITH A VIEW

341 ALFRESCO PIZZERIA AND WINE BAR

St George's Bay
Birżebbuġa
South Malta
+356 2165 3422

A family-run establishment, overlooking small and quaint St George's Bay, that is very popular with the locals, with a great little menu. A good place to relax after a day of swimming, or even to enjoy the sun during the cooler winter months. Alfresco is always busy on the weekends, but other than that no need to book.

No. 341 ALFRESCO PIZZERIA AND WINE BAR

342 COUNTRY TERRACE

Żewwieqa St
Mġarr
Gozo
+356 2155 0248
country-terrace.com

After a day on Gozo, this restaurant, overlooking the busy small ferry harbour that connects the islands, is a great place to stop for dinner. Enjoy the colourful sunsets and panoramic views while you tuck into your delicious dinner.

343 IL TERRAZZO

Triq San Xmun
Xlendi
Gozo
+356 9948 6978

Overlooking one of the idyllic creeks of Xlendi on Gozo, Il Terrazzo combines an excellent location, with good food, and the option of witnessing a mesmerising sunset. Established 20 years ago, this restaurant has continued to change its menu, while maintaining high standards and a reputation for excellent food. Their speciality: fish dishes, of course.

344 INTER-CONTINENTAL BEACH CLUB

St George's Bay
Paceville
Central Malta
+356 2137 7600
intercontinental.com

Part of an international chain of hotels, this restaurant is literally built on the water's edge. The place to enjoy good food, in a relaxing and exclusive atmosphere. The beach club offers access to the beach facilities, and the nearby restaurant. You cannot get any closer to the beach than at the Beach Club.

345 THE PIERRE'S RESTAURANT

Marina Wharf
Marsalforn
Gozo
+356 2156 5727
pierresgozo.com

There are several places in the popular Marsalforn seaside resort, with its rocky beaches and a small sandy beach, where you can enjoy a good meal. At The Pierre's you will be served delicious food, fresh fish, which you are given the chance to choose, with great views across the bay and a nice sea breeze. Booking recommended.

Where the **LOCALS HANG OUT**

---

346 **CAFFE CORDINA**
244 Republic St
Valletta
+356 2065 0400
caffecordina.com

Whatever the weather, this is one of those places that is always teeming with customers, who pop in for a quick espresso and a snack, or for a relaxed drink, in Valletta's main square. The interior is unique, with its early 20th-century paintings and the Italian-style coffee shop. You can enjoy your drinks and snacks outside, in the square, while watching the locals file by. Highly recommended.

347 **DELICATA WINE FESTIVAL**
UPPER BARRAKKA GARDENS
Valletta
+356 2182 5199
delicata.com/
wine-festivals

One of the most popular summer events is the annual wine festival held at the iconic Upper Barrakka Gardens in the first half of August. Besides the excellent and unique view of the Grand Harbour, the music, the atmosphere and the good wine combine to make this one of the highlights of summer, that nobody wants to miss. The wines come from the cellars of the Delicata winery, and you can sample all the premium wines that the winery produces. Admission is free. All you need to do is pay for the wine and food you consume.

348 KINGSWAY

57 Republic St
Valletta
+356 2703 7720
kingsway
valletta.com

Located on Valletta's main street, this bar and cafe references the former name of the street where it is located. Although the interior is smallish, there is ample space beneath the arches, where you can enjoy a cool drink, or even a snack, while enjoying the hustle and bustle of everyday life in the capital city. A great place for some people watching or to unwind after a busy day.

348 KINGSWAY

349 FARSONS BEER FESTIVAL

TA' QALI NATIONAL PARK
Attard
Central Malta
+356 2381 4114
farsonsbeer
festival.com

Farsons, the leading local brewery, organises an annual summer festival at a former airfield, where patrons can drink and taste the company's different beers while enjoying great music by rock and other bands. Admission is free although you have to pay for the beer and food that you consume. This summer celebration attracts hundreds of people every year as it is one of the best outdoor events of the summer in Malta.

350 LA BOTTEGA

200 Merchants St
Valletta
+356 2703 9547

Mornings at this place are quiet, and enjoyable. La Bottega is located in one of the main shopping streets of Valletta, with outdoor seating. During the late evenings the atmosphere changes, with many people gathering here to enjoy some music, the company of friends, and the drinks and food as well. The place to be.

351 MARSOVIN WINE FESTIVAL

HASTINGS GARDENS
Windmill St
Valletta
+356 2182 4918
marsovinwine
festival.com

Another large winery that produces a good range of wine and that holds its traditional wine festival in one of the gardens of Valletta in July. The beautiful setting within the gardens, offering panoramic views of the area beyond the fortified city and Marsamxett Harbour, blends well with the wine and food on offer as well as the great line-up of bands. Admission is free and you only pay for the wine and food that you consume.

DOMUS ZAMITELLO

SLEEP

BOUTIQUE *hotels*

352 CESCA BOUTIQUE HOTEL

2 Xlendi Valley
Xlendi
Gozo
+356 2155 1768
cesca.com.mt

This 18-room hotel, overlooking a still pristine valley, is situated away from the nearby villages. All the rooms have different layouts and views. A new concept for Gozo, it is already proving popular due to its location and serene setting. An excellent place to unwind and get away from the crowds.

353 LA FALCONERIA HOTEL

62 Melita St
Valletta
+356 2247 6600
lafalconeria.com

Every year, the Knights of St John were required to send a single Maltese falcon to Charles V of Spain. This is where the Order's chief falconer once kept, trained and bred these prized birds. The front half of the building dates from the 16th century, whereas the latter was destroyed during World War II and had to be rebuilt. A great place to enjoy the peace and quiet of times gone by.

354 MERCHANT SUITES

191 Merchants St
Valletta
+356 2124 2696
merchantsuites.com

Nestled in the heart of Valletta along one of the city's main streets, this urban boutique hotel offers plenty of comfort and a unique experience. The restyled building is conveniently located near the main historic and cultural sites of the UNESCO World Heritage centre. Classy interiors and comfortable accommodation with helpful staff.

355 PALAZZO CONSIGLIA

102 St Ursula St
Valletta
+356 2124 4222
palazzoconsiglia.com

Located off the main shopping area – but close enough to enjoy the vibrant streets of Valletta –, this modern boutique hotel is situated in a converted traditional townhouse. The amenities are second to none and include a superb spa in the original vaulted limestone cellar, as well as a rooftop pool, overlooking the city's majestic Grand Harbour.

356 THE SAINT JOHN

176 Merchants St
Valletta
+356 2124 3243
thesaintjohn
malta.com

A recent addition to the line-up of boutique hotels in Valletta, this hotel is perfect for exploring the city's culture and heritage. The former merchant's residence and shop have been beautifully restored. The Saint John also has a great little gastropub, with a varied menu. Definitely worth staying at!

357 VALLETTA SUITES

St Lucia St
Valletta
+356 7948 8047
vallettasuites.com

A small, family-run collection of boutique accommodation, catering to discerning travellers and located off the beaten track in Valletta. The four comfortable suites are all named after places and personalities associated with the history of Valletta: Maison La Vallette, Lucia Nova, Valletta Nobile and Corso Cotoner. There are just four suites, ensuring guests enjoy personalised service at all times.

HISTORIC HOUSE *hotels*

358 PALAZZO PAOLINA
101 St Paul's St
Valletta
+356 2124 2442

This 16-room boutique hotel, in the heart of the capital city of Malta, offers the perfect accommodation for well-heeled travellers. Relax by the pool, with a view over the rooftops of Valletta, after a day of exploring the city's palaces.

359 ROSSELLI
167 Merchants St
Valletta
+356 2124 5245
rossellimalta.com

A boutique hotel with lots of history and character, located in the 17th-century residence of a noble family, which has since been restored to its former glory. The Rosselli is situated in Valletta's old town and has an excellent bar and restaurant. Enjoy summer evenings and views of Valletta's skyline by the rooftop pool.

360 XARA PALACE HOTEL
Misrah il-Kunsill
Mdina
Northwest Malta
+356 2145 0560
xarapalace.com.mt

A five-star boutique hotel hidden away in the fortified medieval city of Mdina, the old capital of Malta, with fine restaurants and great amenities. The Xara Palace is situated just off the main street and boasts amazing views of the surrounding countryside and part of the island. Some of the suites have a jacuzzi on the terrace – quite unique.

361 DOMUS ZAMITTELLO

7 Republic St
Valletta
+356 2122 7700
domus
zamittello.com

Located just a short walk from the centre of the historic and UNESCO Heritage city of Valletta, this unique boutique hotel is in a league of its own. The rooms, which are housed in a beautifully renovated 17th-century baroque palazzo, are lavishly decorated and come with all the necessary and modern amenities. Head to the roof to enjoy stunning views of Valletta's city gate, the surrounding baroque buildings, and the city's main street.

361 DOMUS ZAMITTELLO

Stay with **LOCALS**

362 **CUGÓ GRAN HOTEL**

Macina, Triq il-31
Ta' Marżu
Senglea
Southeast Malta
+356 2711 2711
cugogranmalta.com

A hotel that has breathed new life into an old building. Within walking distance of the Three Cities, with stunning views of the marina and the Grand Harbour, the Cugó's elegant interior contrasts with the austere military façade of the 17th-century landmark in which it is housed. The rooftop pool is a great place to unwind. Both the bar and the restaurant are popular with locals.

363 **HOTEL DEL PORTO**

1 Marina St
Kalkara
Southeast Malta
+356 7904 9587
villadelporto
malta.com

Set within the small fishing village of Kalkara, this relaxing retreat is situated across from the bustling marina and a great place to start your visit of the fascinating Three Cities. The area has several good restaurants, while the evenings offer a good opportunity to enjoy the relaxing atmosphere.

364 **LUCIANO AL PORTO**

255 St Ursula St
Valletta
+356 7711 1110
vallettaboutique.com

A well-designed boutique hotel close to all the main cultural and historic attractions and the Grand Harbour. Very handy for the ferry to Gozo too. The modern rooms have retained their old charm. Some of the rooms come with amazing views of the Grand Harbour and the Three Cities.

365 THE EMBASSY VALLETTA HOTEL

173 Strait St
Valletta
+356 2016 9000
*embassyvalletta
hotel.com*

The latest addition to Valletta's boutique hotel scene, it is also the most centrally located, close to all of the city's main attractions. Contemporary, luxurious rooms and friendly professional staff as well as a unique rooftop pool and restaurant: all the ingredients for an enjoyable stay. The rooftop terrace boasts 360-degree views of Valletta and its two harbours.

366 QUAINT HOTEL

13th December St
Nadur
Gozo
+356 2210 8500
quainthotelsgozo.com

One of a chain of small boutique hotels in Malta and Gozo offering exclusive accommodation, usually set in the centre of the village. The Nadur Quaint Hotel is located next to the parish church, overlooking the main square. Here you can observe the locals as they go about their daily business, attend church, or stop for a beer at one of the bars in the square. Boutique accommodation with a twist.

367 SNOP HOUSE

23 Victory St
Senglea
Southeast Malta
+356 2702 9324
thesnophouse.com

Stay in the heart of the city where it's all happening. Located near the church and the main street of this fortified city, the Snop House features superb rooms, with all the necessary amenities. The rooms are all decorated with original artwork, as the owners, who are long-time residents of Malta, are keen art lovers. Each room has its own theme, with a link to Maltese culture, such as the local lace culture or the island's megalithic temples.

368 THE VINCENT HOTEL

84 Old Hospital St
Valletta
+356 9931 5435
thevincenthotel
malta.com

This unique 400-year-old palazzo in the heart of downtown Valletta offers guests a real taste of local life. The city centre is just a short uphill walk from the hotel. Luxury living with all the amenities, away from busy uptown Valletta. The 13 suites all have a quirky, colourful decor.

369 KNIGHTS IN MALTA

138 Triq Santa
Luċija
Naxxar
Northwest Malta
+356 9926 2769

Located in the old village of Naxxar, this small but exquisite guesthouse gives you the option of living like the locals with easy access to public transport to Gozo and Valletta. The nicely decorated rooms are equipped with all the mod cons. Head to the rooftop for a relaxing soak in the hot tub at the end of the day.

369 KNIGHTS IN MALTA

INDEX

COLOPHON

EDITING *and* COMPOSING — Vincent Zammit

FINAL EDITING — Sandy Logan

GRAPHIC DESIGN — Joke Gossé and doublebill.design

PHOTOGRAPHY — Joseph Galea

COVER IMAGE — Fishing village of Marsaxlokk (secret 370)

The addresses in this book have been selected after thorough independent research by the author, in collaboration with Luster Publishing. The selection is solely based on personal evaluation of the business by the author. Nothing in this book was published in exchange for payment or benefits of any kind.

D/2022/12.005/14
ISBN 978 94 6058 2660
NUR 510, 512

© 2022 Luster Publishing, Antwerp
First edition, May 2022
lusterpublishing.com — THE500HIDDENSECRETS.COM
info@lusterpublishing.com

Printed in Italy by Printer Trento.

MIX
Paper | Supporting
responsible forestry
FSC® C015829